THAT SOUERAINE LIGHT

THAT SOUERAINE LIGHT

Essays in Honor of Edmund Spenser

1552–1952

EDITED BY

WILLIAM R. MUELLER

AND

DON CAMERON ALLEN

NEW YORK / RUSSELL & RUSSELL

CONTENTS

I

THE FAÇADE OF MORALITY

By J. W. Saunders

I. *Ambivalence in Tudor Professional Poetry*

The audience the poet *wants* and the audience he knows he will *get* are seldom identical. Usually, he has to look two ways, keeping one eye on the chosen few who will understand his aspirations, and the other on the general public who will not, but who will nevertheless demand their moneysworth. At its most acute, the problem of the conflicting claims of two audiences produces a kind of schizophrenia: Blake and Wordsworth and Shelley, at the beginning of their poetic careers, had dreams of chapbook circulation, of a universal audience, of unparalleled opportunities for the persuasion and enlightenment of mankind; at the end, they were talking to themselves, or conversing in symbols few could understand, or satisfying the hunger of their real middle-class audience for an escape into green hills, faery faraway and long ago. At the least, the problem produces a dualism in the poet's attitude and an ambivalence in his poetry: Chaucer's *pot-pourri* was a dish from which all his readers—the scholars, the courtiers, the merchants, the yeomen—could select their own morsels and enjoy their own favourite flavours; Dryden tried to satisfy both the plain, rational man-in-the-street and the needs of an aureate, Augustan court; Auden writes for the uncommon man, and at the same time keeps the door of his poetry open for the common man by his theories of ' light ' verse. Some dramatists too have faced the same problem: what was Shaw's *primary* audience, his " pit of philosophers," his friends in the little theatre, or the West-End public? Shaw wooed them all with perennial assiduity.

Tudor professional poets were not exceptions to the rule:

1

their particular problem was to reconcile the opposed claims of a Courtly and a middle-class, printed-book audience. Even the *doyen* of them all, Edmund Spenser, was never free; like his colleagues, he too looked two ways. In a recent article, I have discussed the attitude of the Tudor professional poet towards print, and the paradox inherent in it.[1] While he was compelled to seek print to advance his claims to social promotion, he was also eager to look, and write, as much like a Courtier as possible, and he was consequently apt to assume the Court poet's distaste for the publicity of print. But while the poet who ventured into print was apologising, with one hand, to the patronistic, Courtly, manuscript audience for passing beyond its limits, and saving his face, as best he could, from the stigma of print, with the other hand he was conciliating a different audience and a different stigma. The printed book brought poets face to face with a new middle-class audience, to whom they had to justify poetry itself.

Poets in the sixteenth century took care to address their printed-book audience as *learned, courteous* and *gentle*. These adjectives were not meaningless terms: *learned* involved the possession of a University degree or its social equivalent, *courteous* implied a social bearing modelled upon the manners of the Court, and *gentle*, or *generosus*, was a title of respectable social status. But the effort to claim gentility for his audience was on a par with, and as honest as, the professional poet's claim of gentility for himself. The highest possible assumption was made, consistent with the known and unavoidable facts. Doubtless, besides receiving occasional presentation copies, upper-class readers bought, from time to time, books of poetry from the London bookstalls. Certainly, the satellite gentry of the Universities and the Inns of Court might be expected to do so.[2] But private manuscript circulation reduced the need of many

---

[1] "The Stigma of Print," *Essays in Criticism* (April, 1951), pp. 139-164.

[2] The miscellanies seem to have been primarily aimed at the Inns of Court men. Richard Jones, in his address in the *Arbor of Amorous Devices*, lamented that the plague of 1593, when Trinity term had to be adjourned and Michaelmas term kept at St. Albans, hindered his "poore Presse from publishing any pleasing Pamphlet." He wished all in the country a speedy return "to the comfort of all poore men of Trades."

upper-class readers for printed books, and, in any case, the bookstalls were open to the streets, and the printed-book audience was therefore likely to include anyone with sixpence to spare for a book of poems. And poets, in their epistles to their readers, seemed to acknowledge the existence of a wider audience. It is significant that John Grange addressed the *Golden Aphroditis* to the " courtelike dames and ladie-like gentlewomen," the inference being that his dames were not of the Court, nor his gentlewomen ladies (the citizens' wives and daughters seem to be indicated). In the following examples the words which indicate an acknowledgement of a wider audience have been italicized: John Dickenson (*Shepheardes Complaint, ?1594*) addressed " all courteous gentlemen, readers, scholars, and *whosoeuer else affects the studie of poetrie*"; Tailboys Dymoke (*Caltha Poetarum*, 1599) "gentlemen & *others that delight to write*"; James Sandford (*Garden of Pleasure*, 1573) "gentlemen and *others that desire the knowledge of the Italian toung*"; Gascoigne (*Posies*, 1575) " al yong gentlemen, *and generally to the youth of England*"; Richard Johnson (*Nine Worthies of London*, 1592) " the gentlemen readers, *as well prentices as others.*" [3]

The citizen and his wife, his daughters and his apprentices, and the sons he wanted to send to the Universities and the professions, were members of the new, rising middle class, and their literary interests were decidedly not the same as those of the Courtier and the upper-class manuscript audience. Works of piety and devotion or books of psalms and homely didacticism were much more likely to please the London citizen than sonnets of love. An indication of his taste is given by the book-sales of the day. The four best-selling books of verse produced during the entire sixteenth century were the Sternhold-Hopkins Psalter (47 editions 1549-1600), Thomas Tusser's *Good Pointes of Husbandrie* (17 editions 1557-1620), Robert Southwell's *Saint Peter's Complaint* (15 editions 1595-1636), and William Hunnis's *Seven Sobs of a Sorrowful Soule for Sinne* (14 editions

---

[3] Johnson's title-page is also revealing; the book is advertised as being " Pleasaunt for Gentlemen, not vnseemely for Magistrats, and most profitable for Prentises "!

1581-1636) . Even the most popular of the miscellanies, Tottel's *Songes and Sonnettes* and the *Paradise of Dainty Devices*, or popular books like Shakespeare's *Venus and Adonis* and Marlowe's *Hero and Leander*, did not quite approach these figures, and works like Spenser's *Faerie Queene* or *Shepheardes Calender*, which were well above the average in popular esteem, reached a maximum sale of only four or five editions in the poet's own age.

The middle classes, who were the only section of the community large enough to demand the frequent reprintings indicated of the more didactic books, were in the vanguard of the movement towards asceticism in public morality, which was soon to culminate in the establishment of the Commonwealth. Writers in particular were increasingly reminded that the printed page was a powerful weapon, for good or evil, in the struggle to impose sterner standards of public morality. In the first instance the attention of the reformers was directed upon the street ballads. It was Miles Coverdale's aim to use the Psalms to replace " naughty songs of fleshly love and wantonness " so that " women sitting at their rocks, or spinning at their wheels . . . young men also that have the gift of singing, musicians and courtiers " would be better occupied " then with *hey nony nony, hey troly loly* and such like phantasies." [4] This argument is repeated, in virtually the same terms, by John Hall (whose *Courte of Vertue* was a counterblast to the *Court of Venus*, a much read collection of poems by Wyatt and other Courtiers) , Thomas Sternhold, Matthew Parker, Robert Holland, and others. As a result of the pressure of the reformers, the street ballads became increasingly concerned with pointing a moral. After the ballads, the chief target was the stage-plays, the attack being conducted by skilled writers like Stephen Gosson, William Hunnis, John Northbrooke and William Gager.

But poetry of all kinds and the poetic temperament itself was under storm. A typical comment is Bishop Bale's contemptuous reference to the streak of poetry in his friend John Leland:

[4] *Goostly Psalmes and Spirituall Songes (ante* 1539) , preface.

I muche do feare itt that he was vaynegloryouse, and that he had a
poetycall wit, whyche I lament, for I iudge it one of the chefest
thynges that caused hym to fall besydes hys ryghte dyscerynges.[5]

This sort of criticism was widespread. John Wharton, intro-
ducing Jud Smith's *Misticall Deuise*, affirms that it became
Christians to read more wholesome documents than those from
which one was apt to " heare any old bables . . . or stale tales of
Chauser, or to learne howe Acteon came by his horned head."
The term " lying poet " was almost a *cliché* of the day, as
Sidney, Robert Southwell and Gervase Markham reveal. Centuries of scholastic theology had left its deep mark: Tertullian,
Jerome, Boethius, Augustine and Gregory had established the
hostile opinion that, at best, poetry was foolishness in the eyes
of God. In all sorts of ways those in authority tended to reflect,
or make use of, the reactionary views of the reformers. In 1582,
for example, in an age of recultivation of the classics, there
occurred the extraordinary decision of the Privy Council to
recommend that Ocland's Latin verse should replace in schools
that of the " lascivious " and " heathen " classical poets. There
was fundamental hostility to poetry in the minds of influential
people. Nor could Sidney and the other Courtly apologists
provide the radical defence poetry needed. Sidney agreed with
the reformers in contemning the public theatre, the street
ballads, the bawdy sonnets and all the productions of the ragged
rhymers. His motives were partly based upon an awareness of
the need of the Tudor state, cut adrift from the disciplines of
the medieval community, to re-establish a sense of moral purpose and to direct its energies into innocent and laudable activi-
ties, but partly also upon a distrust of all forms of verse which
were intended for wider audiences than the Courtly groups.
At any rate, by insisting upon the divinity, the *dulce et utile*,
the discipline and decorum of good poetry, he confirmed the
art as a wholly upper-class pursuit, and in effect left the enemy
in full possession of their objectives in the printed-book field.

Here was a contributory reason for the deep and sincere
reluctance of the Courtier to allow his poems to pass beyond
the confines of a select and intimate manuscript audience, for

[5] *The Laboryouse Journey,* preface.

whom poetry played an essential part in life. The consequences
for the professional poet, who could not profitably avoid the
publicity of print, were more stern: in addressing the printed-
book audience, he was expected to be the guardian of public
morality. And, since the professional poet was eager to write
Court poetry, and thereby love poetry, he was confronted with
a formidable problem.

English poets, of course, had never been blind to the needs
of public morality. Chaucer had retracted the impiety of *Troilus
and Criseyde*, and rounded off the *Canterbury Tales* with the
Parson's sermon. " Morall Gower " and the " morall vertue "
of Lydgate were potent influences in an age when long serious
works were apt to be more widely read than romances.[6] Even
jolly Skelton found the need to write in the more sombre mood
of *Magnyfycence* and *A Replicatioun*. When Sir Giles Alington,
in a misguided moment, suggested to Barclay that he should
produce a modern version of the *Confessio Amantis*, the poet
refused to " write of thing wanton, not sad but insolent," and
offered his patron instead the *Mirrour of Good Maners.*[7] Hawes
was another poet who would have nothing to do with those who

> .... spend theyr tyme in vaynfull vanyte
> Makynge balades of feruent amyte
> As gestes and tryfles without fruytfulnes.[8]

Another was Henry Bradshaw. Writers, readers and printers
were concerned with the useful, the moral, the didactic and
the pious, a long time before the Puritan movements of the
sixteenth and seventeenth centuries. But, after the Reformation, there were essential differences. The medieval synthesis
had gone and there was no longer an accepted refuge and form
of public repentance in which the poet could without personal
anguish and without the sacrifice of poetry make his peace with
morality. Poets in Tudor times were much more closely engaged
and pursued, and the risks in offence were much greater. Printers

---

[6] Statistical confirmation is provided by Carleton Brown and R. H. Robbins,
Index of Middle English Verse (1943), p. xi.

[7] Ed. Spenser Society (1885), p. 3.

[8] *Vide Passetime of Pleasure*, lines 1317, 1319-23, 1338-41, 1389-93, etc.

were cautious and could refuse to handle work about which there was the slightest suspicion; promotion and social preferment might be denied; the censors had power to burn or ban books, and imprison writers; and, especially in that age of anxiety that came upon professional poets in the last decade or so of Elizabeth's reign, when Daniel, Churchyard, Lyly, Ocland, Peele, Arthur Hall, Henry Lok, Richard Robinson and others testified to the increasing parsimony of patronage, no poet could afford to ignore strong contemporary currents of thought. The printed-book poets were, if anything, even more at the mercy of the middle-class authorities who regulated the London bookstalls than their colleagues of the public theatres.

Poets, then, who wrote for print, were obliged to conciliate the new middle-class audience, and to make peace with its ascetic outlook. A façade of morality was erected to protect poetry from the stigma of folly and worthlessness. But the poets (including the translators into verse) found it more difficult to provide moral justification for their work than other literary men. It was simple for the historian, for instance, so long as he were prepared to adopt an appropriate bias. Stanyhurst was able to assure the reader that

.... In perusing this historie, you shall find vice punished, vertue rewarded, rebellion suppressed, loialtie exalted, hautinesse disliked, courtesie beloued, briberie detested, iustice imbraced, polling officers to their perpetuall shame reprooued, and vpright gouernours to their eternall fame extrolled.[9]

The translators found themselves faced with the more formidable task of representing the pagan poets as keen moralists. Horace, said Drant, " was excellent good in his time, a muche zelous controller of sinne, but chiefly one that with sharp satires and cutting quippies, coulde wel displaie and disease a gloser." [10] Drant does not seem to have been altogether content with this claim, for, to reinforce the moral façade, he published with the translations from Horace, the *Wailings of the Prophet Hieremiah*. Similarly, Abraham Fleming felt obliged to discover a

[9] Stanyhurst's own dedication to Sir Henry Sidney, printed before his contribution to Holinshed's *Second Book of Chronicles*, 1586.
[10] *A medicinable Morall* (1566), " To the reader."

hidden allegorical significance in Virgil's *Eclogues*. Even Ovid, it was believed, displayed moral purpose. Thomas Peend gravely declared that his Pleasant Fable of *Hermaphroditus and Salmacis* was a moral work, particularly concerned with "that fylthy lothsome lake of lust" which takes the "strengthe from lusty men," and the "mad desyres of women, theyr rage in folysh fits." And Arthur Golding, who translated the whole of the *Metamorphoses*, insisted that

> With skill, heede and iudgement, this worke must be read,
> For else to the Reader it standes in small stead.[11]

But, as one of his descendants has pointed out, " Golding was apparently dissatisfied with his failure to impress Elizabethans with the fundamental ethical purpose that he saw in the *Metamorphoses*, for he never again translated a classic that in any degree bordered on the immoral or improper. In fact he did not translate any other classic for ten years, and at that time he did the unexceptionable work of Seneca." [12]

The love poet was compelled to distort his material in the same way. The commonest moral excuse for love poetry was that given by J. C's friend " Philaretes ":

> Let me entreate you to suffer these your Passionate Sonnets to be published, which may peraduenture make others possessed with the like humor of Louing, to follow your example in leauing, and to mooue other *Alciliaes* (if there be anie) to embrace deseruing loue, while they may.[13]

Love poetry, all else failing, could always be represented as a public confession of folly for the moral good of young readers. Thus, Gascoigne defended the least moral of his poems of 1573 as "a myrrour for unbrydled youth, to auoyde those perilles which I had passed." [14] And, in response to the censorship exercised by the Court of High Commission, he divided his poetry into " Flowers, Hearbes and Weedes." The blushes of the love poet were, naturally enough, more profuse than those

[11] *Op. cit.* (1575), title-page.
[12] L. T. Golding, *An Elizabethan Puritan* (1937), p. 55.
[13] *Alcilia*, 1595, repr. A. B. Grosart, 1879.
[14] *Poems* (ed. J. W. Cunliffe, 1907-10), I, 4.

of his colleagues. William Averell was so perturbed that the public might consider his *Life and Death of Charles and Julia* too immoral that he frankly urged those who were shocked by it to burn it by the candle with which they read it!

Possibly the most violent distortion of poetic purpose was presented by the young soldier, Arthur Broke:

> And to this ende (Good Reader) is this tragicall matter written, to describe vnto thee a coople of vnfortunate louers, thralling themselues to vnhonest desire, neglecting the authoritie and aduise of parents and frendes, conferring their principall counsels with dronken gossyppes, and superstitious friers (the naturally fitte instrumentes of vnchastitie), attemptyng all aduentures of peryll, for thattayning of their wished lust, vsyng auriculer confession (the kay of whoredome and treason) for furtheraunce of theyr purpose, abusying the honorable name of lawefull mariage, to cloke the shame of stolne contractes, finally, by all means of vnhounest lyfe, hastyng to most vnhappye deathe.[15]

His poem *mirabile dictu* was the version of *Romeus and Iuliet* that inspired Shakespeare's tragedy of star-crossed lovers. Fortunately, this preface is only a moral façade; in reality, the poem was a pleasantly told tragic romance devoid of any face-saving moral veneer. Romeus, Broke declares in the poem, is actually " free from fowle desire," Juliet refuses " wanton loue " and an " unlawfull sute," and Fryer Lawrence is " not as the most .... a gross vnlearned foole," but a doctor of divinity, a man of beauty and wisdom, beloved and honoured of all, who in the end

> .... was discharged quyte, and no marke of defame
> Did seeme to blot or touch at all the honor of his name.

And, far from condemning the lovers, Broke confesses

> I graunt that I enuie the blisse they liued in:
> Oh that I might haue found the like, I wish it for no sin.
> .... Of shyuering care and dred I haue felt many a fit.
> But Fortune such delight as theyrs dyd neuer graunt me yet.

At the end the bodies of the lovers are given a stately tomb

> Lest that length of time might from our myndes remoue
> The memory of so perfect, sound and so approued loue![16]

[15] *Romeus and Iuliet*, 1563, repr. *Originals and Analogues*, Pt. I (ed. P. A. Daniel, New Shakespere Society, 1875), preface.
[16] *Ibid.*, lines 578 ff., 2999 ff., 903 ff., and 3111 ff.

The preface must indeed have been written *after* the poem, in order, that is, to provide a moral façade for the book on the stalls.

If the consequence of the necessity to conciliate the middle-class audience had been limited merely to the obligation to protest a moral purpose in the prefaces of books, the critical relevance would have been slight. But there were more insidious effects. Many professional poets were, in fact, *put in two minds*, both about the general purpose of poetry and about their own poetic aims. Some poets reached the point of publicly retracting their work and " resigning " from the profession. The dramatists, with a greater independence and security, despite all kinds of interference by the City authorities and their frequent experiences of prison, were reasonably immune, but even so Gosson found it profitable to turn quisling on his colleagues, Lodge stopped writing plays altogether, and Fulke Greville destroyed some of his plays to save them from the disgrace of public performance. With the non-dramatic poets the retractation was a common occurence. Gascoigne, who experienced more than most the keen edge of criticism and interference, was so cowed by his experiences with the *Posies* that thereafter he wrote only didactic poetry, the *Glasse of Gouernement*, the *Steele Glas*, and other slighter poems in the same vein, or didactic prose like the *Droome of Doomes Day* or *A Delicate Diet for daintiemouthde Droonkardes*.[17] Thomas Lodge, who abandoned the stage in 1589, wrote a prose work in 1596 entitled *Prosopopeia*, in which he declared the hope that now " at last after I haue wounded the world with too much surfet of vanitie, I maye bee by the true Helizeus, cleansed from the leprosie of my lewd lines, & beeing washed in the Iordan of grace, imploy my labour to the comfort of the faithfull." [18] And thereafter

[17] In these works he did his best to impress his reformation upon his readers. He told the Queen, for instance, in his *Hermit's Tale*:

Beholde here, (learned pryncesse) nott Gascoigne the ydle poett, wryting tryfles of the green Knighte, but Gascoigne the Satyricall wryter, medytating the Muse that may express his reformacion. Forgett (most excellent lady) the poesies which I haue scattered in the world, and I vowe to wryte volumes of profittable poems, wherewith your maiestie may be pleased.

Poems (ed. J. W. Cunliffe, 1907-10), II, 477.

[18] Dedication to the Countess of Derby.

he wrote nothing but medical treatises, translations of Seneca and Josephus, and a summary of du Bartas, although he lived on until 1625. Again, Gervase Markham, who never recovered from being called a " poetycall lying knave " by his kinsman Thomas Markham, came to mourn the sin of " howers mispent in *that* feather-light studye . . . . with as greate hartynes as ever I greeiued for any sinne com*m*ytted gaynst the hyest." [19] Thereafter, he wrote only prose or religious verse, published anonymously under his initials. Turberville bade a farewell to poetry in the closing lines of the *Tragic Tales* in these terms:

> Wherefore, goe (wanton) trusse vp all your trash
> Fancy farewel, to grauer gods I goe,
> Then loue and Venus, cleane my handes I wash,
> Of vayne desires that youth enrageth so
> Vertue doth farre surmount such filthy vice
> Amend my mates, or els you know the price. . . .

Instances of other retractations are numerous. Nicholas Grimald, loath to appear before a printed-book audience as the writer of Courtly amorous lyrics, withdrew, in the few weeks that elapsed between the first and second editions of Tottel's *Miscellany*, all except his didactic verses. Richard Edwards publicly regretted the follies of his early verse.[20] Thomas Underdown in riper years came to consider it " meeter to publish notable examples of godly christian life, then the most honest . . . . historie of love." [21] Thomas Howell deliberately reprinted the more didactic of his poems, though in quality they were inferior to some of his others.

The consciences of other poets led them to add in the printed editions captions and arguments to point the moral of particular poems. There are instances of expurgations: Timothy Kendall, translating Martial, proclaimed " I haue left the lewde, I haue chosen the chaste. I haue weeded away all wanton and woorthlesse woordes." [22] Some poets turned their backs on Court poetry and produced books specifically intended to meet the

---

[19] *The Teares of the Beloued, &c.* (ed. A. B. Grosart, 1871), p. 15.
[10] *Vide Damon and Pithias*, prologus.
[21] Referring to his *Heliodorus* (ed. W. E. Henley, 1895), p. 4.
[22] *Flowers of Epigrammes* (repr. Spenser Society, 1874), p. 9.

demands of middle-class ascetic taste for the pious and didactic. New types of didactic books appeared: collections of psalms, moral miscellanies like *Hunnie's Recreations*, full of " godlie and compendious discourses " on Biblical subjects (versifiers like Fleming, Anne Wheathill, Elizabeth Grymeston, and others, imitated Hunnis's model); " emblem " books, like Geoffrey Whitney's, captiously emphasising the need to establish laws of public morality; chapbooks and broadside-poems of repentance and Christian resolve, like Luke Hutton's; the fashionable last verses of the doomed and martyred, or " Tear " poems on the pattern established by Southwell; centuries of divine sonnets —by Henry Lok, Barnabe Barnes, and others—parodying the secular Petrarchan fashion introduced to manuscript audiences by Sidney and Greville in the 1570's; compendia of good advice and Biblical abridgements, like Edmund Elviden's *Closet of Counsels*; and the educational histories, like John Partridge's *Plasidas*, which were the forbears of the later encyclopedias of moral and political science, like Spenser's *Faerie Queene*.

From poetry, as from other forms of literature, the Tudor middle classes who formed the backbone of the printed-book audience expected not graceful social communication but edification. A sixpence spent on poetry was expected to yield its worth of moral value. This demand increasingly determined the direction and content of contemporary literature. The consequence was that there was a sharp division in literary taste and sensibility. True poetry was of importance only with the Courtly manuscript audience, while the art was adjudged completely unimportant by the middle-class printed-book audience who accepted doggerel, so long as the matter was didactic. Poetry was confirmed as the *amateur* occupation of the few, so that the rise of a literary profession was inevitably directed into other channels. Writing for the stage, though it had its difficulties, was at least less discouraging than writing for the press, and the attractiveness of the public theatre for the young Wits is understandable. It is little wonder that the Tudor poet who ventured into print, with the stigma of social impropriety on one cheek, and the stigma of moral folly on the other, should present such a sorry, timorous and blushing picture. Nor is it inexplicable that so much Tudor professional poetry, full of stylistic and egotistic bombast designed to impress, and full of hypocrisies of representation intended to conciliate both a Courtly and a middle-class audience, should be, with few exceptions, so utterly unnatural and insipid and worthless. Nor is it extraordinary that, again with so few exceptions, the best professional poetry of the period was to be found, not in print, but on the stages of the Globe, the Fortune and the other public theatres. All this the stigma of print and the façade of morality helps to explain.

II. *Spenser's Dualism*

It is little wonder that the professional poets were in two minds, doubtful whether to pursue the tastes of the Courtier and the potential patron, in search of social preferment, or whether to write for the middle-class audience, with whom the future of professional literature presumably rested. Most of the better writers—Spenser, Daniel, Drayton, Churchyard, Gascoigne, Watson, Warner—sought a compromise and tried to please *both* audiences. The consequence was a dualistic attitude, a dichotomous form of poetry, and ethical ambivalence —with far-reaching effects upon the poets themselves and their work. Spenser's career, in particular, was shaped by his determination to please both audiences.

Unlike the nineteenth-century Romantic, Spenser never allowed his natural literary predilection for visions and dreams to interfere with a shrewd, calculating regulation of his poetic career. Like all the Wits, he achieved his first reputation by the circulation of poems in manuscript. With his patrons' susceptibilities in mind—he tells Harvey in a letter dated October 1579 —he did not seek print, " least by ouer-much cloying their noble eares, I should gather a contempt of myself, or else seeme rather for gaine or commoditie to doe it, for some sweetnesse that I haue already tasted." But, by 1579, the time was ripe to further his career by the publication of one selected manifesto of his ability: " Whiles the iron is hote, it is good striking, and mindes of nobles varie as their estates." Not only did he wish to broaden the scope of his patronage, but he intended to extend his political influence in the widest possible field in London.

True to his times, Spenser desired not only poetic fame but a position of political responsibility under the Crown. *The Shepheardes Calender* was the poem selected to further these ambitions. His success was phenomenal: he became the ' new poet ' everybody talked about. Professional writers admired his skill: Nashe called him the " miracle of wit " and Webbe " the rightest English poet that ever I read." Scholars, like Harvey, purred with approval for his learnedness. The book sold well in the stalls and doubtless proved an excellent " almanac " for the middle-class audience. Even the Courtiers noticed Spenser's arrival. Puttenham, who was not always ready to name a professional writer, recorded the new poet in the *Arte of English Poesie* on the strength of this one book. Friendly Sidney was moved to express the cautious opinion that there was much poetry in him, " indeede worthy the reading if I be not deceived." Spenser's ability to win and hold a simultaneous popularity with several different audiences is by far the outstanding mark of his career. To his death, he remained " our principall poet," retaining the unanimous favour of different critics, Richard Barnfield the wit, Richard Carew the squire, Francis Meres the hack, John Chamberlain the dilettante, Robert Allot the middle-class printer, and many others. Why was this so? How did Spenser manage to be, simultaneously, the Critic's poet, the Poet's poet, the Citizen's poet, apparently satisfying every formula, and achieving the encyclopaedic feat of a universal audience?

The answer is that, in poetry intended for print, Spenser deliberately set out to write at different levels of taste and meaning for all his potential audiences. The Eclogue not only provided a form classically appropriate, as E. K. suggests, for young poets to " trye theyr habilities " and " proue theyr tender wyngs," but permitted the writer to make of his poem a *potpourri*, like Chaucer's *Canterbury Tales*, the different ingredients of which made different appeals to different sections of the audience. E. K. divided the Eclogues into " three formes or ranckes . . . . Plaintiue . . . . or recreatiue . . . . or Moral," a grouping which itself gives an indication of different audiences.

Some of the poems were clearly intended for a middle-class audience—*Februarie, Maye, Iulye,* and *September*—those which are didactic, full of moral doctrine, fables, homilies, simple allegories and a quota of ecclesiastical polemics, written in simple metres, either loose accentual, after Chaucer, or " poulter's measure," owing nothing to Continental Renaissance influences. In these poems, Spenser is the voice of the middle-class rank-and-file and of the political Protestantism with which they associated themselves. Other Eclogues were equally clearly intended for the Courtier and his cultured satellites. *Ianuarye* and *Iune* are vehicles for the pseudo-Petrarchan lover, and others are literary exercises in learned modes and Courtly fashions: *March* an attempt at the classical idyll, *Aprill* at a panegyric for the Queen, *August* a singing-match offering experiments in the roundelay and the Petrarchan *sestina*, and *November* a Courtly elegy. These poems, and their metres, undoubtedly had more influence than the others among Courtly writers. It is in *October* that Spenser most closely imitates the Courtier, in talking to himself about himself and the problems of living, and it is here, significantly, that we find autobiographical material about the two Spensers, the idealistic Piers, the professional poet whose ultimate target is the epic, and Cuddie, the greater realist, the satellite poet of the Court.

All his readers must have been well content. The citizenry found good value for their sixpences in the moral gravity, the polemical message, and the eminently quotable homilectic didacticism. Robert Allot's anthology of quotations, *England's Parnassus,* (1600), testifies to Spenser's golden qualities for the commonplace-book keeper: there are nearly 400 quotations from Spenser, whilst his nearest rival, Drayton, is quoted 225 times and Shakespeare only 95. If there were any doubts about the citizen's goodwill towards the almanac, Spenser dismissed them by his moral façade, the claim that the more Courtly poems—those least acceptable to the middle classes—were written " to mitigate and allay the heate of his passion, or els to warne (as he sayth) the young shepheards.s. his equalls and companions of his vnfortunate folly."

The scholars in Spenser's audience could not have doubted

the new poet's learning and culture. Spenser gave them all
the evidence they needed that he knew his Virgil, Mantuan.
Petrarch, Marot and Ronsard, for his book was a pantechnicon
of allusions to other pastoral poetry.[23] He satisfied the patriots
among them by not neglecting to read the crude efforts of
English forbears like Barnabe Googe. His dialect forms, archaisms, borrowings and coinages were the product not of a rash
innovator but of a seasoned scholar for whom E. K. could claim
"auctoritie," since his diction was "both English, and also
vsed of most excellent Authors and most famous Poetes."[24]
"His dewe obseruing of Decorum euerye where" prevented any
outrage to scholarly taste. His rhetoric, highly important to a
University eye, was highly skilled and utterly unexceptionable.[25]
The last charge that could be levied at Spenser by a learned
audience was that he was an ignorant balladist.

What of the Courtly audience? The *Calender* was decidely
not, on the whole, Courtly poetry, which at its best was egotis-
tical, dramatic, restricted to the short lyric, and arising from
day-to-day experiences at the Court, the heart of life. Spenser's
shepherds do not belong to life anywhere, least of all at the
Court. Spenser makes a clumsy attempt to associate them with
the real countryside, but such realism as is given them only
makes ludicrous nonsense of the general fiction. When they
pursue Cupid with "pumie stones" and a "fowling net," or
hie homewards fast when "it gynnes to mizzle," or express fear
of their stepdames "as whott as fyre," or discuss the sovereign
remedy of "Terebinth good for Gotes," it is difficult not to
agree with Dr. Johnson that "Eglogues meant to express the
talk of goatsherds, though it will only mean the talk of goats."
For all their occasional homeliness these shepherds never lived
in any real world. Courtly Arcadias, on the contrary, despite
the artificial fiction, were at least peopled with Courtly folk and
Courtly problems. An additional source of disquiet to the
Courtier was the diction which was most certainly not "the

---

[23] The best account of the precedents he studied is given by W. W. Greg, *Pastoral Poetry and Pastoral Drama.*

[24] Spenser's careful literary skill is the burden of the argument of B. R. McElderry, Jr., "Archaisms and Innovation in Spenser's Poetic Diction," *PMLA*, 1932.

[25] *Vide,* V. L. Rubel, "Poetic Diction in the English Renaissance," *PMLA*, 1941.

usuall speach of the Court ": " that same framing of his stile,"
said Sidney, " to an old rustic language, I dare not alowe, sith
neyther Theocritus in Greeke, Virgill in Latine, nor Sanazar in
Italian did affect it." But Sidney's somewhat pedantic criticism
—which Spenser could have answered by quoting unexceptionable literary precedent—reveals the dilemma in which the
Courtly critic stood. When Spenser expostulated " Why, a Gods
name may we not have the kingdom of our language? ", Sidney
was too gracious, and too cautious in public, to make the real
complaint that Spenser's verse, abnormal and outlandish as it
was, lacked the finish and *raison d'être* of Courtly songs and
sonnets, and he therefore had to be content with a literary
quibble which masked his true objection. And the Courtier,
compromised by the necessity to defend poetry against its
ascetic critics, had publicly committed himself to the claim that
the best poetry ought to be didactic, *dulce et utile*, patriotic,
practised and proficient, decorous in degree, and divinely skilled
in invention. These very qualities—acceptable to the middle-
class audience as well—Spenser had laboured to provide, thus
disarming the Courtier's most damaging objections.

An even deeper distrust must have been aroused at Court by
Spenser's brash cocksureness:

> Loe I haue made a Calender for euery yeare,
> That steele in strength, and time in durance shall outweare:
> And if I marked well the starres reuolution,
> It shall continewe till the worlds dissolution.

No Courtier dared claim, like the almanac writers, this sort of
immortality and *divina vis*. He would have naturally con-
temned this bumptious upstart who thrust among his betters,
and, into the bargain, presented his poems with all the bravado
of an annotated text. But Spenser was adept in anticipating
hostile opinion: just as he erected a moral façade before the
Courtly poems to placate a middle-class audience, so he saved
himself from a Courtly stigma by disguising his professionalism
and self-advertisement under the mask of gentility. The con-
venient fiction of publication by his friend, E. K., and the con-
cealment of his identity behind the pseudonym *Immerito*, not
only made possible a discreet advertisement of the excellences

of the work for both discerning and undiscerning readers, but also provided Spenser with an alibi against any charge of personal *braggadoccio*. These devices, added to the poet's own undeniable virtuosity and ingenuity and Sidney's friendly support, explain why the Courtier's objections must have been effectively silenced.

The diplomat in him deserved to succeed! On the credit side, his promotion to a position of some responsibility in Ireland must be attributed directly to the effect of the *Shepheardes Calender*. That Spenser did not make more of his opportunity, once it was presented, was the fault not so much of any failure in ability or industrious devotion, but of the untimeliness and tactlessness of the political enthusiasms he espoused. The country was not ready for the extreme policies he advocated. This fact, coupled with his misfortunes in patronage—Sidney died young, Leicester was too conservative, Raleigh, and later Essex, were too volatile for the Queen, all alienated the powerful Burghley—makes it apparent that Spenser would have been happier in his politics and in his patronage fifty years later.

Spenser's literary career falls into two overlapping halves: a first period, ending about 1591, in which he interested himself almost entirely in manuscript poetry and gradually acquired a wide circle of Courtly patrons, and a second decade, the period of the *Faerie Queene* and of his printed poetry. Much of his early verse remained in manuscript and has been lost for ever. He printed only the *Calender*, a deliberate exception to the rule, the undergraduate *Visions* written for John Vandernoodt, and the whimsical rag-bags of the common-room, entitled *Three Proper, and wittie, familiar Letters* and *Two other, very commendable Letters*. But the *Faerie Queene* marks a change of policy towards the printing of everything that he wrote. He was no longer content to let his poems find their own market in due and decorous course. In this later period, to save himself from the stigma of print, he elaborated various defensive strategies. He allowed Ponsonby to take the blame for the publication of the *Complaints* in 1591 and to make the claim that the poems had been collected by various means, some having been " disperst abroad in sundrie hands, and not easie to bee come by, by himselfe " and others " diuerslie imbeziled and purloyned from him, since his departure ouer Sea." Ponsonby later claimed to have published the *Amoretti* on his own responsibility in the poet's absence. Spenser himself put forward a moral pretext for the publication of the *Fowre Hymnes*: the necessity " at least to amend, and by way of retractation to reforme " the Hymns to Love and Beauty, many copies of which were " scattered abroad," poisoning young men and women with their " affection." But, despite all these and other defensive devices, the fact remains that by 1589 Spenser was ceasing to pretend to be the amateur dilettante. Before 1589, he would not print even political satire like *Mother Hubberds Tale*; after that year, he was prepared to rewrite it especially for a printed-book audience. It is no coincidence that so much of his poetry of the last decade consisted of " meditations of the worlds vanitie, verie graue and profitable."

The key to his change of attitude is explicit in poems like *Colin Clouts Come Home Againe*, in which he condemns the poet who goes to Court as a fool and forcibly rejects Court poetry and the " vaine votaries of laesie loue ":

> . . . . all the walls and windows there are writ,
> All full of loue, and loue, and loue my deare,
> And all their talke and studie is of it. . . . .
> Ne any one himselfe doth ought esteeme,
> Vnlesse he swim in loue vp to the eares.   (776 ff.) .

At some time in 1589, possibly with the added incentive of a new patron in Raleigh, Spenser decided to make a fresh, uninhibited bid for social preferment by printing the books already written of his brain-child, the *Faerie Queene*, dedicated in his own name to the Queen herself. The proof of his determination to broaden the scope of his patronage lies in his unprecedented multiple dedication, in seventeen sonnets, to all the important leaders of the Privy Council and the Court. And, if this bold policy failed, Spenser knew that a remaining hope rested in the influence he could exert through reaching a wide middle-class audience. This time, Spenser's success was not all he wished. He received, after some delay, a pension of £50 a year which, added to his estate and appointments in Ireland, enabled him to live in reasonable comfort, and his gateway to patronage was widened, especially among the ladies, but his chief target, a political appointment at Court, was denied him. For the rest of his life, as his hopes at Court withered, he fell back, more and more, on his printed-book audience, who welcomed the *Faerie Queene* in successive editions and proved in the end his surest political allies.

From the *Faerie Queene* onwards Spenser wrote, without reprieve, for two audiences simultaneously. The problem of dualism, which he had mastered by a *tour de force* in the *Shepheardes Calender*, recurred in a greater degree of complexity. It was not possible to resolve, again, the conflict of Courtliness and Didacticism in any *pot-pourri*. In any homogeneous poem, Spenser's purposes were irrevocably split in two; and this is why the *Faerie Queene* itself fails in essential unity and is seldom more than a pageant of successive brilliant scenes, without, as Spenser himself feared, a continuous intention preventing tedium and confusion.

Allegory not only permitted Spenser to simulate the gravity of a medieval, romantic pattern, to publish ecclesiastical polemics in assimilable and impeccable form, and to devote himself to the luxuries of his own imagination, it enabled him to convey simultaneously several levels of meaning for different audiences. On a first level, there was the romantic story; on a second level (for his middle-class readers) a moral, political or ecclesiastical lesson; on a third level (for general readers at Court) historical and personal identifications; and on a fourth (for the Courtly readers who truly loved poetry) the imaginative experience itself. The middle-class readers, content to recognize Justice in Artegal, Courtesy in Calidore, and Reckless Honour in Timias, and heartily in agreement with the poet's polemics against the Papists and his advocacy of an austere set of moral values, could hardly have been expected to follow the myriad of identifications and glancing allusions in the historical allegory. The Courtier, however, not only recognising that Essex was Calidore, that Grey was Artegal, and that Raleigh was Timias, but enjoying the more recondite identifications of Mary Stuart with Amoret, the Duke of Anjou with Braggadoccio, and the Countess

of Essex with the graceful Pastorella, would have been considerably less interested in the conflict of morality conceptions. The
dichotomy of the moral and historical allegories is a relatively
less serious problem; another lies far deeper. The unique wonders
of the imaginative experience (and these represented Spenser's
chief claim to genius and poetic fame) and the didactic truths
of the moral allegory are like oil and water; they cannot co-exist
at all in the way that, it can be said, a historical and a moral
allegory can co-exist. Here was the fatal crux for Spenser's
artistry.

Spenser believed, like Sidney, that a poem (even a long one)
ought to have an organic unity. This the mere framework of
the narrative (the device of the twelve days of the Queen's
" Annual feaste " which the poet was so anxious to explain to
Raleigh) could not of itself provide. The sum total of the
imaginative impressions of the poem have to present a unity
too. Thus, Langland's many allegories fuse into a complex unity
which cannot be realised as a whole until due weight is given
to the interdependent yet separate parts of the meaning.[26]
Spenser's difficulty was that the imaginative experience and the
moral lesson to be derived from the *Faerie Queene* pointed to
entirely opposite poles of meaning.

For one reader (the discerning Courtier) the poem was
veritable Fairyland, where *anything* might happen on the next
heath, in the next forest or in the next castle. Good, it is true,
always prevailed over Evil, as it does in a juvenile adventure
story, but ordinary moral values do not obtain. The more impressive the task set the hero, the more dangerous or seductive
the adversary, the more exciting the pursuit, the more imagination is fired. For this reader the secret of the enjoyment lay not
in the invulnerability of the hero but in the exciting problem
itself and the delight was reinforced by Spenser's depth of
imaginative creativeness. This pleasure was not a mere, shallow
interest in the story. On the contrary, at its best, the *Faerie
Queene*, to this reader, held the same charm (same in degree,
but not in extent) as the expanded conceit which was the heart
of Elizabethan poetry: the whole was an extravagant, outrage-

---

[26] Cf. Mr. Eliot's problems in the *Cocktail Party*.

ous, incredible metaphor of the individualist taking arms against a sea of troubles. But to the next reader, the sober but unimaginative citizen, the poem was a mere lesson in which Good was predestined to overcome Evil and its whole point was the invulnerability of virtue and the inevitably corrupting consequences of vice. The poem was, it is true, an encyclopedia of the virtues and vices, but, to this reader, at its best, it was as simple as a handbook. Neither of these readers could have been entirely content with the poem as it is: to one, the successes of the hero would have been sometimes disappointingly facile and unilluminating, the extrications from his predicaments too often the work of an arbitrary *deus ex machina*, while to the other, at times, the vices would have appeared too attractive and seductively decorative, the virtues so unnecessarily imperfect.

Spenser recognised the dilemma. In his letter to Raleigh, he confesses that *while*

> The general end therefore of all the booke is to fashion a gentleman or noble person in vertuous and gentle discipline: Which for that I conceiued shoulde be most plausible and pleasing, being coloured with an historicall fiction, the which the most part of men delight to read, rather for variety of matter, then for profite of the ensample. . . . .

at the same time

> . . . . many other aduentures are intermedled, but rather as Accidents, then intendments. As the loue of Britomart, the ouerthrow of Marinell, the misery of Florimell, the vertuousnes of Belphoebe, the lasciuiousnes of Hellenora, and many the like.

That is to say, while his chief aim was to erect a sensuous façade to " colour " the moral doctrine, he confesses that, at times, his interests are waylaid by sensuous pleasure.

> The waies, through which my weary steps I guyde,
> In this delightfull land of Faery,
> Are so exceeding spacious and wyde,
> And sprinckled with such sweet variety,
> Of all that pleasant is to eare or eye,
> That I nigh rauisht with rare thoughts delight,

My tedious trauell doe forget thereby;
And when I gin to feele decay of might,
It strength to me supplies, and chears my dulled spright.

(VI. 1)

Again and again, it is the *moral* purpose which becomes tedious
and enervating to him, and it is to his sensuous Fairyland that
he clings as his real source of pleasure and inspiration. At such
times, a façade of morality has to be erected to protect himself
from the criticisms of his ascetic readers. A particularly significant example occurs at the beginning of Book IV, the first lines
published in the 1596 instalment:

The rugged forhead that with graue foresight
Welds kingdomes causes, and affaires of state,
My looser rimes (I wote) doth sharply wite,
For praising loue, as I haue done of late,
And magnifying louers deare debate;
By which fraile youth is oft to follie led,
Through false allurment of that pleasing baite,
That better were in vertues discipled,
Then with vaine poemes weeds to haue their fancies fed.

But, he goes on to declare, love is the root of honour and virtue,
and a source of philosophy:

Witnesse the father of Philosophie,
Which to his *Critias*, shaded oft from sunne,
Of loue full many lessons did apply,
The which these Stoicke censours cannot well deny.

(IV, 3)

As long as he pleased the Queen (and, by inference, the Court),
he was content with such façades. As long as he had any hopes
of social preferment at Court, it was likely that the audience
most sympathetic to his imaginative creations would provide
support for his own instincts, and that Fairyland would prevail.

The conflict between the *dulce* and the *utile* went deep into
Spenser's heart. His favourite word was " delight " and his
favourite technique the sensuous metaphor, but his moral and
political creed was austere and ascetic. When an inherent contradiction like this was reinforced by the claims to attention of
two different audiences, the dilemma must have been acute;

at any rate, it influences every part and aspect of the poem. The outlines of the allegories often become blurred. In the latter half of Book VI, his chief subject is officially the " atchieuement of the *Blatant Beast*," but his jaded imagination lingers so long in the shade with Pastorella,[27] that the Beast in the end has to be summarily despatched in a few stanzas. From a *moral* viewpoint, this pastoral digression reveals the social and moral ineptitude and futility of the lazy shepherds, contrasted with Calidore's superior Courtesy. Thus, Coridon is routed in one throw and turns coward when Pastorella and her friends are in danger, while Calidore, single-handed and virtually unarmed, twice rescues the Lady. Meliboeus and his friends are doomed to annihilation, whence only Pastorella is reprieved. But from an *imaginative* viewpoint, this golden world is a source of repose and refreshment not only for Calidore, but for Spenser *and* his readers, and the Knight is quite the dullest of the inhabitants. Spenser escapes from the dilemma by arranging the identification (by a happy mole) of Pastorella as the long-lost daughter of Lady Claribell, and therefore as of Courteous blood. Thus, at the eleventh hour, the most delightful of his ladies was levered, somewhat clumsily, into a niche in the moral allegory, which otherwise she would have falsified and negatived.

As with the story, so the descriptions, the metaphors and the very vocabulary of the poem are continually at cross purposes with the moral allegory. Fundamentally, Spenser was the imaginative poet in love with the drama and fire and excitement of his own creation, and his moral earnestness comes second best. His love for the sensuous evocations of colour and light images is an important example. His virtues and vices always parade in masques of conflicting colours, dazzling whites and guilty blacks, fertile golds and costly scarlets, and the moral and symbolical values attached to them tend to disappear, beneath the transforming power of his imagination, until only the sensuous brillance remains vital and vivid and semantic in a context of fantasy far removed from moral truth.

Spenser attempts, in his colour imagery, to marry, in one impression, medieval symbolism and a particular moral attitude,

---

[27] His conscience reminds him of his error: *vide* x 1, xii 2, etc.

to descriptive accuracy and imaginative evocativeness. But in
such a marriage the imagination bullies the moral symbol into
complete submission. His reds (with the golds, by far his
favourite colours) exemplify the problem. Red was the colour
of Blood, and therefore symbolises *War* (the Red Cross of
the Knight), *Life* (Diet is " yclad in red "), *Anger* (hence
Pyrochles's " sandy lockes . . . knotted in bloud," and Furor's
" tawny beard " and " long lockes, colourd like copper-wire "),
and *Youth* and *Freshness* (the rosiness of cheeks, lips, blushes,
fruit and the Dawn). But Red was also the colour of Fire,
and redness, flaming and burning, blazing and glowing, symbolises also the *Purifier* and *Destroyer*. Further, the redness of
Scarlet, in particular, signified *regal luxury* (Una's Court is
" bespred with costly scarlot " and Britomart in her dream
perceives her linen changing into a royal robe of scarlet), and
the connotations in this sense were often, as with Duessa and
Malecasta, evil, for Scarlet was the cardinal colour of Rome.
In many instances, it is true, the particular symbol selected from
these multiple meanings is determined by the context, but the
brillance of the colour image itself drowns, as often as not, the
moral overtones.

> Now whenas all the world in silence deepe
> Yshrowded was, and euery mortall wight
> Was drowned in the depth of deadly sleepe,
> Faire *Malecasta*, whose engrieued spright
> Could find no rest in such perplexed plight,
> Lightly arose out of her wearie bed,
> And vnder the blacke vele of guilty Night,
> Her with a scarlot mantle couered,
> That was with gold and Ermines faire enueloped.   (III. i 59)

What is indelible in this picture is not the scarlet of Rome, or
the guiltiness of Night, or the deadliness of sleep, but the
exciting, luxuriant flash of red and gold against the night sky
of lovers.

The commonest connotation of gold, to Spenser, was its
glitter. The moral values of the colour derive from the directly
opposite meanings of ' worth.' In a bad sense it implies the
flamboyant wealth and luxury of Lucifera, Duessa, Mammon
and the Lady of Delight, and in a good sense the splendid

nobility of Phoebus, Prince Arthur, Charissa or Belphoebe. Often the immediate context is unhelpful in deciding the exact symbolical value of the colour. When Lucifera is described, on her " rich throne, as bright as sunny day," as

> A mayden Queene, that shone as *Titans* ray,
> In glistering gold, and peerelesse pretious stone.   (I. iv 8)

we have to read on to discover that she is Pride, with a dreadful Dragon at her feet, and that no comparison with Elizabeth was intended, at least consciously, by the poet. When Prince Arthur appears,

> His haughtie helmet, horrid all with gold,
> Both glorious brightnesse, and great terrour bred;
> For all the crest a Dragon did enfold
> With greedie pawes, and ouer all did spred
> His golden wings. . . .   (I. vii 31)

we have to read further to discover that this Knight (and his Tudor dragon) are on the side of Virtue. In these contexts, the imaginative excitement and colour-brilliance completely overthrows the moral allegory which limps along behind very much as an afterthought.

Yellow is used by Spenser as an associate of gold, especially with regard to hair. All Spenser's heroines are blondes: Una, Pastorella, Belphoebe, Florimell, Aurora, Medina, Alma and others. Yellowness, in medieval literature, always symbolised *fertility*; and, thus, with Charissa,

> Her necke and breasts were euer open bare,
> That ay thereof her babes might sucke their fill;
> The rest was all in yellow robes arayed still. . .   (1. x 30)

and in the Mutability Cantos it is Autumn who is clad in yellow. But Spenser often contradicts this basic symbolism. Some of his blondes are vowed to virginity, and some, like the maidens in the Bower of Bliss, to wantonness, so that, as often as not, the golden hair is no more than a conventional mark of beauty (as it still is in modern films and pantomimes). When Spenser's golds and yellows really impress, it is a pretty picture that they evoke, not a moral value.

Silver is, to the poet, chiefly the symbol of *Truth*. The Red
Cross Knight has a silver shield and in the white silk robes of
Una silver is intertwined. But when Radigund is depicted in
a purple " Camis "

> Wouen vppon with siluer, subtly wrought,
> And quilted vppon sattin white as milke.   (V. v 2)

and Acrasia, of all people, is also found to be wearing silver,
we can only conclude that, once more, imagination has van-
quished the symbolism. The silverness of *sound* (of Belphoebe's
voice, for instance) does not always imply goodness, for there
is a silver fountain in the Bower of Bliss. And the pale brillance
of the colour, especially in descriptions of moonlight, is quite
amoral.

One would imagine that the traditional connotation of white
as the colour of *purity* and *innocence* would without any difficulty have outweighed for Spenser any descriptive or evocative
value. But this is not so. Fidelia, and Alma " araied all in lilly
white " are, it is true, innocence incarnate. But whiteness was
also, to Spenser, the colour of a beautiful woman's naked skin,
and the poet seeks all kinds of similes—of lilies, snow, ivory,
pearls, milk and alabaster—to intensify his descriptions of her
attractiveness. Belphoebe's cheeks are like " roses in a bed
of lilies," and Shamefastnesse's snowy cheeks her became " as
polisht iuory." In his romantic eagerness Spenser sometimes
achieves ecstasies of hyperbole. Una rode

> Vpon a lowly Asse more white then snow,
> Yet she much whiter, but the same did hide
> Vnder a vele, that wimpled was full low,
> And ouer all a blacke stole she did throw.   (I. i 4)

As for Florimell,

> A fairer wight did neuer Sunne behold,
> And on a palfrey rides more white then snow,
> Yet she her selfe is whiter manifold.   (III. v 5)

These are sensuous studies in black and white, and gold and
white, rather than symbolical pictures. Spenser could achieve

similar hyperboles in his descriptions of evil women, like, for instance, Acrasia, whose whiteness is all seductiveness and impurity:

> Vpon a bed of Roses she was layd,
> As faint through heat, or dight to pleasant sin,
> And was arayd, or rather disarayd,
> All in a vele of silke and siluer thin,
> That hid no whit her alablaster skin,
> But rather shewd more white, if more might bee.   (II. xii 77)

The sensuous titivation here makes even Sin " pleasant."

With all the other colours there is a similar conflict between the moral and the sensuous values. The sudden blacks (often in similes of pitch, sable, coal or jet) symbolise *Evil, Death, Grief,* and *Poverty,* but the effectiveness of the colour in contrasts with brightness is often more important to Spenser than the moral value. Blue represents *Fidelity, Timidity* (used in a good sense with Shamefastnesse), *Cowardice* and *Fear* (Duessa's blue eyelids), but Spenser is so often excited by the music of the word " azure " and by similes of flower-blueness (especially violets) that the moral allegory is forgotten. Green is much more often the colour of Fairyland's wonderful woods and pastures than the symbol of *Disloyalty* or *Novelty.* The poet's *primary* concern at all times was for the imaginative possibilities of colour evocation. He never uses the plain cardinal term of red, yellow or blue, if he can avoid it by an imaginative synonym. The illuminant quality of his colour words was more important to him than the pigment itself. And the deepest values of his poem spring from his brilliant ability to draw pictures of light and shape and colour in sculptured tableaux, patterned tapestries and glorious pageants.

Yet, even though at times it were no more than a façade, we cannot ignore the decidely retarding influence exerted upon his imagination by a moral allegory which he could never afford totally to neglect. To this poet, whose chief excellence was his visual imagery, Sight was the most sinful of the senses. When Guyon is tempted by Money in the dungeons of Mammon, or by Beauty in the Bower of Bliss, it is through the eyes—rebuked by the Palmer as ' hungry,' ' greedy,' ' wandering '—that the sin enters his soul. Spenser's heroes and heroines, good and evil alike, never seem to gaze or stare—they peep and espy, as if looking itself were wicked. Spenser's own eyes seem to waver between a surrender to sensuousness and an awareness of moral law with all the enthusiasm and the timidity of a Peeping Tom. The moralist displays an extraordinary, and in the circumstances a morbid, interest in nakedness. His lovers (even Venus and Adonis) always enjoy each other in the thickest coverts of secret arbours; yet, again and again, Spenser arranges interruptions when bashful intruders suddenly surprise coy nakedness. Guyon's discovery of the " two naked Damzelles " in the Bower of Bliss, Calidore's intrusion upon Serena and her " iolly Knight " in " couert shade," and even Venus's sudden surprisal of Diana and her maidens bathing at the fountain, are all opportunities specially created for the sensuous description of nudes, in which the very vocabulary of bashfulness serves a double purpose. In these contexts, and others like them, words like ' dainty ' have sexual connotations:

> Two naked Damzelles he therein espyde,
> Which therein bathing, seemed to contend,
> And wrestle wantonly, ne car'd to hyde,
> Their *dainty* parts from vew of any, which them eyde. . . . .
>   (In the Bower of Bliss, II. xii, 63)

> Sitting beside a fountaine in a rew,
> Some of them washing with the liquid dew
> From off their *dainty* limbes the dustie sweat. . . . .
>   (Diana and her maidens, III. vi, 17)

> So forth they rode, he feining seemely merth,
> And she coy lookes: so *dainty* they say maketh derth. . . .
>   (Seduction of the Red Cross Knight by Fidessa, I. ii, 27)

> Vpon the banck they sitting did espy
> A *daintie* damzell, dressing of her heare. . . .
>   (The wanton Phaedria, II. xii, 14)

All the fastidiousness in the Bower of Bliss—" *dayntiest* fantasie," " the most *daintie* Paradise on ground," melodious sounds to " delight a *daintie* eare," Genius " *daintily* . . . . deckt with flowers," and so on—conveys not neatness but the tempting titivation of the sexual appetite. Other words descriptive of pleasure—*sweet, pleasant, merriment*, even *delight* itself—carry sexual overtones. It is implicit, in this vocabulary, that Spenser enjoyed his sensuous pictures, and explicit that he was conscious of their sinfulness. His maidens blush in coyness, but the demure are seldom what they seem. For all his earnestness, his delight in his own creations turns the moral allegory, so often, into a mere façade.

A sense of humour, that saving grace which enabled Chaucer to look on the human scene without inconsistency, could not rescue Spenser in his dilemma, for no one laughs in the *Faerie Queene* except at pornography or deformity. The laughter of the Knights led by the Squire of Dames when all the pretentious women failed to don Florimell's girdle, the amusement of Satyrane at the Squire's failure to find a chaste woman, the provocative sniggers of the naked Damzelles in the Bower of Bliss—this is the only laughter in the poem, for, unlike Blake, Spenser believed that even Mirth was sinful. In his Court poetry, the poet allowed himself an occasional wry smile, with his tongue in his cheek:

> Enough it is for one man to sustaine
> the stormes, which she alone on me doth raine. . . .
>
> What then can moue her? if nor merth nor mone,
> she is no woman, but a sencelesse stone. . . . .[28]

At these moments, the dryness of the wit that mocks his own Courtly extravagance puts him nearer the vein of Donne than at any other point in his poetry. Or, again, in purely professional poetry, like *Colin Clouts Come Home Againe*, Spenser reveals that he does possess some sense of humour. But in the poems which were written for two audiences, even the occasional flicker of amusement was totally extinguished.

It was almost a forlorn task to attempt, as Spenser did, to yoke together sensuousness and moral earnestness in one allegorical unity. How can a poet surrender himself to, for instance, a Fairyland of brilliant colours, when all the time one part of him is convinced that colour itself was sinful? Under the influence of the Platonic doctrine of mutability, the theory of the inevitable decay of all outward forms, Spenser recognized that

---

[28] *Amoretti,* sonnets **XLVI** and **LIV.**

the very wealth of natural colour was, at best, a snare and a delusion, and, at worst, utter moral poverty. The very word ' colour ' or ' colourable,' perhaps by analogy with the rhetorical term, has a bad sense.

> What man so wise, what earthly wit so ware,
> As to descry the crafty cunning traine,
> By which deceipt doth maske in visour faire,
> And cast her colours dyed deepe in graine,
> To seeme like Truth? (I. vii, 1)

Spenser tried to draw a distinction between false colours and the true. Duessa had the gift of changing

> .... her former wonted hew:
> For she could d'on so manie shapes in sight,
> As euer could Cameleon colours new;
> So could she forge all colours, saue the trew. (IV. i, 18)

Thus, the poet declared all *unnatural* colours to be evil: Error's blood is coal-black, Duessa's giant is a purple beast, Pyrochles's steed is bloody red, Eurytion's kine are purple, and the fruits in the Garden of Proserpina are black. *Variegated* colours (probably from the analogies of the proud peacock and the evanescent rainbow) are also evil: the Dragon in Book I is " bespotted as with shields of red and blacke," and the Monster in Book III is " Monstrous mishapt, and all his backe was spect With thousand spots of colours queint elect." *Artificial* colours, too, are evil: Philotime's was not " her owne natiue hew But wrought by art and counterfetted shew," and the word' painted ' invariably spelled moral turpitude. But, despite these arbitrary rules, Spenser was unable to maintain a consistent attitude. Duessa's alchemy had no limitations at all: she, and the other temptresses in the poem, could forge and wear even the purest whites and the most fertile golds. No colour was safe from the protagonists of Evil.

As the poem progresses, Spenser seems to become more perplexed by his dilemma, and more hesitant in his colours. Mr. J. B. Fletcher has demonstrated that there are fewer than half as many colour and light images in the last three books as in the first three.[29] As he remarks, " to turn at once from the reds

---

[29] " Some Observations on the Changing Style of the Faerie Queene," *Stud. Phil.*, XXXI, 1934.

and golds, the radiant lights and the deep shadows of Book One, to the grey half-lights of Book Six, is to experience two different sense-worlds." The decline is general from the luxuriant frequency of colour and light images in Books I and II to the barest incidence in Book VI, but the most significant difference occurs between Books III and IV, that is to say, between the books printed in 1590 and 1596. Whatever other reasons there may be for this decline—Mr. Fletcher suggests that a less frequent use of compound adjectives and an increase in narrative speed would proportionately denude the poem of colour luxuriance—between the writing of the first three books and the writing of the last three Spenser must have experienced a change of attitude towards the sensuous imagery that formed the heart of his Courtly poetry. In these very years Spenser's concern for his own material welfare had altered with a growing disillusion about the opportunities available for Courtly preferment. In these circumstances, his eagerness to please a Courtly audience must have been diminished, and more force must have been given to other considerations, in particular, the emphasis placed on moral didacticism by the printed-book audience. The choice lay between the poet's own sensuous imagination and a Courtly audience, on the other hand, and his earnest conscience and a middle-class audience, on the other. In his early poetry he chose the former; but, ultimately, the latter won.

On the whole, his best poetry was written for the Court. His audacious ' pantechnicon ' conceits:

> Her lips did smell lyke vnto Gillyflowers,
>   her ruddy cheekes lyke vnto Roses red:
>   her snowy browes lyke budded Bellamoures,
>   her louely eyes lyke Pincks but newly spred.
>
> Her goodly bosome lyke a Strawberry bed,
>   her neck lyke to a bounch of Cullambynes:
>   her brest lyke lillyes, ere theyr leaues be shed,
>   her nipples lyke yong blossomd Iessemynes.
>
> Such fragrant flowres doe giue most odorous smell,
>   but her sweet odour did them all excell;
>
> *(Amoretti,* LXIV)

his antitheses of demure sensuousness:

> Sweet is the Rose, but growes vpon a brere;
>   Sweet is the Iunipere, but sharpe his bough;
>   sweet is the Eglantine, but pricketh nere;
>   sweet is the firbloome, but his braunches rough.
> Sweet is the Cypresse, but his rynd is tough,
>   sweet is the nut, but bitter is his pill;
>   sweet is the broome-flowre, but yet sowre enough;
>   and sweet is Moly, but his root is ill   (*Amoretti*, XXVI)

and his ability, in passage like these, to fuse a Renaissance organic unity with a Medieval catalogue; his gift for the marri-. age of rhetoric and ritual with pagan clarity:

> Woods, hills and riuers, now are desolate,
> Sith he is gone the which them all did grace:
> And all the fields do waile their widow state,
> Sith death their fairest flowre did late deface,
>   The fairest flowre in field that euer grew,
>   Was *Astrophel*; that was, we all may rew.
>
> What cruell hand of cursed foe vnknowne,
> Hath cropt the stalke which bore so faire a flowre?
> Vntimely cropt, before it well were growne,
> And clean defaced in vntimely houre.
>   Great losse to all that euer did him see,
>   Great losse to all, but greatest losse to mee;
>   (*Astrophel*, 241-252)

his haunting lyricism:

> They gathered some; the Violet pallid blew,
> The little Dazie, that at euening closes,
> The virgin Lillie, and the Primrose trew,
> With store of vermeil Roses,
> To decke their Bridegromes posies,
> Against the Brydale day, which was not long:
>   Sweet *Themmes* runne softly, till I end my Song;
>   (*Prothalamion*, 30-36)

all these excellences, his very finest, have their happiest opportunities in the poetry which originates in a Courtly audience and a Courtly purpose. When his poetry is adulterated with the dualism of two audiences and two purposes, it was burdened with a loss not only of clarity but of fertile inspiration itself.

The dualism, especially of the *Shepheardes Calender* and the *Faerie Queene*, is responsible for the two Spensers who have always been opposed in critics' eyes. W. B. Yeats looked into the " shadows of a joyless earnestness " and chose the " poet of the delighted senses." [30] Mr. C. S. Lewis balanced the Elfin, Renaissance, Voluptuous, Courtly, and Italianate Spenser against the English, Protestant, Manly, Churchwardenly and Domestic.[31] Emile Legouis weighed the allegory against the intellectual activity of the age, and settled for the " innate voluptuousness " of the poet whose imagination was haunted by his visual experience.[32] The dualism has been apparent ever since Rymer and Temple and other Augustan critics first drew the distinction between, on the one hand, Spenser's flights of fancy and marvellous adventures, and, on the other hand, the didacticism and the gilding of the pill. Spenser's contradictions are part of his temperament: he was *both* the poet of militant Protestantism and the writer of medieval allegory, *both* the hard, shrewd administrator and the man of delicate susceptibilities, *both* the cultured Classical poet and the first, exuberant Romantic. But these temperamental contradictions might have been wholly reconciled except for the fundamental dilemma of the Courtly satellite who sought print to advance his fame, and was thenceforward enthralled between the Scylla of Courtly sensuousness and the Charybdis of middle-class asceticism. Poetic schizophrenia and breakdown must have been the inevitable fate of the *Faerie Queene*, had Spenser lived long enough to persist with it. Not even the mightiest aggregation of ladies riding out of bushes on white palfreys, noble Knights hewing helmets into pieces, monsters gushing forth black blood from deep wounds, could have saved the poem from the dualism of an unquenched ambition which sought to serve two masters at once. Where morality was the heart, sensuousness was the façade; where sensuousness the heart, morality was the façade; and never the twain could meet in any lasting unity.

York, England

---

[30] *The Cutting of an Agate*, 1902.
[31] *The Allegory of Love*, 1936.
[32] *Spenser*, 1926.

II

"ETERNE IN MUTABILITIE":
THE UNIFIED WORLD OF *THE FAERIE QUEENE.*

By Kathleen Williams

To give unity to so complex a poem as *The Faerie Queene* would seem a formidable task, and it was a task which Spenser left unfinished. Our loss, in the six unwritten books, is great; and all the greater because of the cumulative method by which the poem's meaning is revealed. The later books enrich the content of those which have gone before, so that from the first book to the fragmentary seventh the reader becomes increasingly aware of a clear and comprehensive vision, and of a steady purpose which impels him, through a mass of significant detail, towards a final unity.

That unity, at the court of Glory herself, was never reached, and without the unwritten books our appreciation of those we have must be incomplete. But even as it stands, half-finished and culminating in the fragment of the presumed seventh book, the poem is a unified whole. For the kind of unity which Spenser achieves, though cumulative, is not architectural; he works not by adding section to section so that the structure is meaningless until it is finished, but by revealing new levels of a structure which we thought complete at our first sight of it. Faeryland is only partially revealed, but it is unified and consistent as far as we know it, though if the poem had been completed it would be seen as only part of a greater unity and a fuller truth. The first book of *The Faerie Queene* has a simplicity which is proper both to its theme and to the plan of the poem; Spenser begins at the centre of his universe, with the proper conduct of man in relation to God, and the link which still exists between the world of mortality and the realm of eternal truth. Book II. shows, almost as simply, the control which is a necessary part of the good life. Themes so essential must be firmly and directly established, but in later books the concern is less exclusively with man, and the natural world too plays its part. Around the centre other and related themes appear, making a richer and more complex whole.

Yet Spenser's method is not a matter only of decorum or deliberate choice. As with any great poet writing seriously about the nature of man and of the universe, his method arises directly out of his vision. An eighteenth century poet, like Pope, will find it natural to write in contrasts, extremes whose balance will produce a truth more central than either. Spenser too sometimes uses a set framework of the Aristotelian mean and its two corresponding extremes, and finds it on occasion a useful piece of machinery; but it is not, as with Pope, his most natural way of seeing things. The living world of *The Faerie Queene* is not one of contrast and balance, but of analogy and parallel, with many kinds of life each complete in itself yet only fully comprehended when seen in relation to the rest. The full poetic effect cannot be contained in Spenser's own statement to Raleigh, " The generall end therefore of all the book is to fashion a gentleman or noble person in vertuous and gentle discipline." Man holds a place of prime importance in Spenser's vision of the world, but the conduct proper to mankind cannot be divined by looking at man alone. The other planes of existence must be comprehended too. So Spenser's is not a simple allegorical world of black and white, concerned only with the " twelve morall vertues as Aristotle hath devised." There are degrees and kinds of goodness, and these can be seen only when all the parallels are drawn, all the analogies completed. Allegory may present an ideal of moral or political conduct, but beyond a certain point the reader must, to apprehend all of Spenser's vision, yield to the deepening effect of the poem as a whole. The Aristotelian framework and the allegory of the virtues, the vices, the parts of the mind, form a pattern; one may fit together into a satisfying unity the various kinds of chastity as shown in Belphoebe, Britomart, Amoret, and Florimell. But there is another and more organic pattern, resulting from the inevitable ordering of the material in accordance with Spenser's way of seeing the world, and developing from book to book to a temporary culmination in the Cantos of Mutability. In this pattern, the shape of the poem is part of its meaning, while characters like Belphoebe and Florimell are symbols which release certain aspects of Spenser's apprehension of life, and cast about them " shadows of an indefinable wisdom."

Much of the significance of *The Faerie Queene* is conveyed in the correspondences and parallels which are gradually established throughout the poem, and of course in the choice of symbol; and in both it is the Platonic rather than the Aristotelian influence on Spenser's mind which is most noticeable. For a poet so much in tune with Neoplatonism it is natural to express not personal reactions only but an interpretation of the universe by means of symbol. " All things that are above are here below also," and material things which more or less embody the Ideas are themselves already latent symbols of those Ideas. Spenser is always conscious of things as deriving from, and partially embodying, their heavenly counterparts, and as bound together by their common derivation, their common if varying possession of ideal truth. Chastity lives in heaven, but is embodied and displayed in each chaste woman. Shamefastness exists as the fountain of Guyon's modesty, and is not a mere abstraction formed by generalising the modesty of many individuals, as so often in the personifications of later ages. Courtesy, like all virtues, grows on Parnassus, but its " heavenly seedes " were planted on earth, while as a copy among men of this heavenly process the Queen is an ocean of courtesy, from whom all virtues proceed to those who surround her, and to whom they return as rivers to the sea.

Such an outlook enables the poet to see about him a multiple unity which is embodied in the development of his poem. There is no division between literal and symbolic truth, for things exist in an order of precedence which is valid in itself, but they have at the same time a symbolic validity as imperfect copies of the world of spirit from which they take their source. In *The Faerie Queene* events are never merely events; they partially show forth something beyond themselves. Spenser's battles, it has often been remarked, have less variety of incident and less actuality than Ariosto's or Tasso's, but Spenser is interested in something else. Tasso's Dudon strives three times to raise himself before he dies, and there is a gain in suspense and dramatic climax, but when Red Crosse falls three times to rise

again during his fight with the dragon Spenser is concerned less
with the dramatic effect of the particular event than with the
greater struggle of which it is a shadow. The four-fold repetition
of " So downe he fell," at the death of the dragon is again not
only dramatic, it is a solemn ritual repetition meant to empha-
size not the size of a dragon but the terror of sin even at the
moment of its defeat:

The knight himselfe even trembled at his fall.   (I, xi, 51)
Symbol and allegory, often difficult to separate, are especially
so in Spenser's case, for he often uses the same figure now as
part of a moral or political allegory, now as a symbol of an
indefinable truth. His characters move freely from one plane to
another, or exist simultaneously on more planes than one, and
that existence is at once both a means of unifying the poem and
a symbol of the multiple unity of the world which—among other
things—the poem expresses.

Occasionally Spenser makes use of incidents or figures which
might support the definition of allegory quoted by W. B. Yeats: [1]
" Symbolism said things which could not be said so perfectly
in any other way, and needed but a right instinct for its understanding, while Allegory said things which could be said as well,
or better, in another way, and needed a right knowledge for its
understanding." The giant of false justice, in Canto II. of Book
V., is such a contrived and limited figure, fitting one occasion,
but not suggesting others. But the Giant, and those like him,
serve to throw into relief the far greater number of creatures
in *The Faerie Queene* who, like Wordsworth's monumental
shepherds and travellers, hint at the terrible greatness of the
events of this world. Nothing exists in isolation, but draws
with it an immense but controlled suggestion of other occasions
which are yet the same. Another of the figures of Book V., the
deceitful Malengin who harries Mercilla's kingdom, may refer
to the guerilla warfare and treacherous behaviour of the Irish,
but this falsity is a part of, and a symbol of, all deceit. The
chase and the traditional beast transformations suggest the old
menace of the covens, and even the primal deceit of the devil;
for Malengin is killed as he changes into a snake, and his
dwelling goes down to hell.

---

[1] In " Symbolism in Painting," *Ideas of Good and Evil.*

Malengin is one of the representatives of that evil which
devil and man have brought into the world, and evil is shown
here, as so often in Spenser, as deceit. Like the giant Orgoglio,
who vanishes when Prince Arthur kills him, it is based upon
nothingness, upon a false view of things. It tries to break the
unity and shatter the truth of the universe, but it is doomed
to defeat, for "Truth is One in All," and against that solid
truth, present in some degree throughout the created world,
evil can have no lasting force. It is seen as an alien intruder
into the world of reality, and is embodied in the evil spirits
which are used to make the false images of Una and Florimell,
or in the devilish Malengin, Despair, and Archimago. To the
clear sight of complete virtue it is irrelevant, but to a lesser
goodness it is formidable indeed, for it is part of man's inheri-
tance, making impossible for him the innocence of the natural
world, and present in man alone. Nature may be involved in
the fall and the suffering of man, but not through its own fault.
It is only through the presence of a fallen angel that the snow
which makes the false Florimell is corrupted.

The world of *The Faerie Queene* is one in which the values of
Neoplatonism and of Christianity are familiarly blended, and of
course it is very far from being peculiar to Spenser; but it is
expressed in his poetry with a particular vitality. What other
poets must show in the flash of an image, Spenser develops
through the six Books of *The Faerie Queene* into a living and
consistent universe. Through the growing pattern of the poem
can be traced levels of being which extend from pure intelli-
gences to inanimate nature, distinct but related by their common reference to the guiding and informing spirit which gives
unity and order to a multiple world. It is not a dual world of
pointless change contrasting with eternal changelessness; the
changing world derives from, and returns to, unity, and each of
its levels is good in its degree, being a reflection of the eternal.
In ascending scale, created things are more beautiful because
more pure—clearer manifestations of the spirit which informs
them:

> Still as everything doth upward tend,
> And further is from earth, so still more cleare
> And faire it growes, till to his perfect end
> Of purest beautie, it at last ascend.   (H.H.B., 43-47)

But though distance from the home of pure spirit, and involvement in matter, must lessen the purity and beauty of the creatures at certain levels, all have their beauty and in Spenser's symbolism their goodness. All

> are made with wondrous wise respect,
> And all with admirable beautie deckt,   (H.H.B., 34-35)

and in no part of Spenser's universe is the hand of God absent. His providence sustains and guides even the apparently lawless world of the beasts and the apparently 'aimless world of inanimate nature, but in this orderly universe springing from and guided by God the disruptive and unruly element is man. Spenser writes in Book V. of the

> impotent desire of men to raine,
> Whom neither dread of God, that devils bindes,
> Nor lawes of men, that common weales containe,
> Nor bands of nature, that wilde beastes restraine,
> Can keepe from outrage, and from doing wrong.
>
> (V., xii, 1)

Other created things are restrained by the laws proper to their being, and when Spenser considers evil the emphasis is, here as in *An Hymne of Heavenly Love,* on the sin of man, rather than on any sinfulness inherent in the whole material world. Our " sinfull mire," in which we endure fleshly corruption and mortal pain, is part of the inherited frailty of fallen humanity.

> We all are subject to that curse,
> And death in stead of life have sucked from our Nurse.
>
> (VII., vi, 6)

Amavia, telling Sir Guyon the story of her husband's submission to Acrasia, accepts it as part of the weakness of man when faced by temptation through fleshly lusts:

> For he was flesh: (all flesh doth frailtie breed).
>
> (II., i, 52)

The same emphasis appears in the myth of Chrysogone and her two children. In the world of humanity, conception is involved in the " loathly crime " of the fall; but Chrysogone conceives in all the lustless innocence of the natural world, without sin and without pain:

> Unwares she them conceived, unwares she bore:
> She bore withouten paine, that she conceived
> Withouten pleasure.   (III., vi, 27)

Her children are born of sunshine and moisture, sharing the
purity which characterises all the natural world when uncon-
taminated by the inherited sin of human flesh. Belphoebe is

> Pure and unspotted from all loathly crime,
> That is ingenerate in fleshly slime,   (III, vi, 3)

but Amoret too shares in the innocent birth, and the fruitful
Garden of Adonis in which she is reared is presumably as much
a symbol of primal innocence as are the cool chaste forests
through which Belphoebe ranges.

The innocence and even holiness of nature, when considered
without reference to the contamination of sin in the case of
humanity, is one of the most noticeable features of Spenser's
world, but there is nothing of that sentimental idealisation of
the " natural " to which a later age was to fall victim. Spenser's
clear vision of the ascending planes of existence prevents any
loss of proportion, any concentration on a part of life to the
detriment of the rest. The satyrs of Book I. are innocent and,
in their degree, good. Only the sacredness of the old religious
rites is shown in their worship of Una, and they are an instrument of " eternall Providence exceeding thought," an example,
like the noble lion of natural law who is killed by Sansloy, of
the guidance of God even in the non-human world. But this is
not the whole truth about the satyrs, for there is a parallel
picture in Canto 10 of Book III., where Hellenore, garlanded
like Una, is escorted by a similar band of dancing satyrs. Here
the word used is not, as in Una's case, " queen," but " May-
lady," and in the scenes which follow the license of the old
nature cults, which the word suggests, is fully revealed. The
satyrs have not changed; they are still charming, innocent, a
" lovely fellowship," but Spenser is looking at them from a
different point of view, and drawing an exact parallel with Una's
story to make clear both the likeness and the difference in their
good and our own. Hellenore is capable, as a human being, of
a higher and more conscious goodness than that of the innocent
brute world, and in entering that world she misuses it just as,

with Paridell, she had misused the natural goodness and the
sacred symbolism of wine.

There are many of these lesser planes in *The Faerie Queene*,
and Spenser shows them in themselves and in relation to man.
In forests and above all in the sea, we are shown kinds of being
which, good in themselves, are not proper to mankind. The seas
and forests are unknown, lacking by human standards in morality and in spirit. They can contain creatures of non-human
goodness, like Belphoebe, but those who go there from man's
world—Hellenore, the forester who pursues Florimell, the fisher-
man who attacks her—become brutalised. But nature, even
at its most remote from man, has its share of the spirit which
is the meaning of Spenser's world. The mutable is not neces-
sarily the meaningless, but can " work its own perfection so
by fate." What is meaningless and dead is the work of sin, of
pride and distorted values, the places of Mammon or of Malecasta, where the lifeless glitter of gold and jewels is shown up
in all its emptiness by the sudden reference to the stars in their
order, reflections of mind and symbols of the steady life of the
spirit,

> th' eternall lampes, wherewith high Jove
> Doth light the lower world.   (III., i, 57)

It is, then, a universe with varying degrees of good, and evil
which is a distortion, or sometimes a subtly distorted copy, of
the good: the unnaturalness of Argante, Ollyphant, and the
" damned souls " who capture Serena, or the magic and deceit
of Acrasia, Duessa, and the false Florimell; and it is revealed
partly by the gradual accumulation of correspondences between
one kind of life and another. There are parallels between Una
and Hellenore, Mercilla and Lucifera, the Garden of Adonis
and the Bower of Bliss, Cleopolis and the New Jerusalem, the
veiled Venus of Book IV. and the goddess Nature of Book VII.
The virtues are seen, more and more, as various aspects of
the same heavenly good, embodied in different ways in different
kinds of life. " Truth is one in All," or to put it in another way,

> O goodly golden chaine, wherewith yfere
> The vertues linked are in lovely wize.   (I., ix, 1)

It is not a matter only of interlinked stories or of characters

overlapping from one book into another. It is a linking, by
symbol and allegory, of Justice with Constancy, Love with
Courtesy; a deepening of content by reference to earlier themes
so that nothing is lost, and so that certain passages, pre-emi-
nently the Mutability Cantos, can call up by the briefest of
references the more detailed treatment of earlier books, drawing
all their diversity into unity.

One of the most far reaching of Spenser's series of inter-linked
and expanding symbols is that of Florimell and Marinell, which
stretches through three books and embraces many meanings
and many characters. In the moral allegory, it is a story which
displays Spenser's knowledge of humanity, and of the various
temptations to which different natures will be subject. Florimell
is one kind of chastity, the kind which maintains itself not by
the awe which Belphoebe and Britomart inspire, but by fear
and flight. Her temptation is not, like Amoret's, passion, but
a timorous softness and gratitude. She escapes from her brutal
pursuers by instinctive flight, but is disarmed by the protective
kindness of Proteus, to be imprisoned by him as Amoret is
imprisoned by Busyrane. On the same level of moral allegory,
Marinell's is the nature which refuses to commit itself, and
lives remote and self-sufficient, fearing the harm which may
come to its own completeness by contact with others. But
they are, both of them, more than this, for they play an important part in the network of symbol. Both seem to be creatures
of the natural world which stands apart from the life of men
but which yet, such is the unity of things, has its relevance to
that life as it has to the life of pure spirit. The sea which is
so intimate a part of their story is the remotest of all things
from man, home of hydras and " sea-shouldring whales," and
yet it is the most perfect of all symbols for the whole multiple,
changing, but unified world, " eterne in mutabilitie." The sea
can symbolize the character and meaning of the universe and
so embodies a truth beyond itself, but it stands also, in its own
right, for nature at its least formed and most nearly chaotic.
It can show the thoughtless, blameless cruelty of nature, its
blind suffering, and also the justice which works through it as
through all creation. Such meanings play through the story of
Marinell and Florimell, and the other stories which surround it,

drawing even the Fifth Book, in which the justification of one
man and one policy plays so large a part, into the scheme of
the whole.

We meet first Florimell, " beautie excellent " and of a kind
which delights the world,

> For none alive but joy'd in Florimell,   (IV., ii, 23)

but apparently of a lesser order of being than that to which the
great champions of virtue belong. Britomart, usually so prompt
to relieve distress, refuses to join in the pursuit of Florimell,
and she is clearly right. Britomart's

> constant mind,
> Would not so lightly follow beauties chace.   (III., i, 19)

She remains faithful to her search for Justice and noble deeds,
one aspect of that quest for ideal goodness to which her companions also, Guyon, Arthur, and Arthur's squire Timias, are
in their various ways committed. In abandoning their quest,
these others are leaving their proper sphere of spiritual endeavour, constancy to an unchanging truth, to pursue the fleeting
charm of a mutable world. As a result, even the steadfast Prince
Arthur finds himself at the mercy of passing events and emotions, and is perceptibly a lesser figure during this period of
pursuit. Forgetting for the moment his vision of Gloriana, the
true object of his quest, he gives way to confused fancies, wishing
that Florimell were the Faerie Queene:

> And thousand fancies bet his idle braine
> With their light wings, the sights of semblants vaine:
> Oft did he wish, that Lady faire mote bee
> His Faery Queene, for whom he did complaine:
> Or that his Faery Queene were such, as shee:
> And ever hastie Night he blamed bitterlie. (III., iv, 54)

After a night of sleepless irritation, Magnificence itself becomes
almost petulant:

> So forth he went,
> With heavie looke and lumpish pace, that plaine
> In him bewraid great grudge and maltalent.
>
>   (III., iv, 61)

Florimell's innocent beauty is too nearly empty of meaning for man to be other than harmful to high endeavour. She has little understanding of what is happening to her, but flies instinctively and suffers blindly, with the infinite uncomprehending pathos of nature. She has no place with the knights and ladies who represent human virtues but encounters, rather, creatures of nature like Satyrane and Proteus, and brutalized human beings who try to make use of her for their own ends. Yet this pathetic, fugitive creature, embodiment of transitory beauty, has her own element of constancy; her desire for union with Marinell, who is born of the sea, symbol of the source and home of all changing things.[2] Her long flight and her suffering begin and end in her love for Marinell, and her story has its meaning, though to the world of men, of Arthur and of Britomart, it may seem to have none. Florimell's story is a parallel to that of Amoret, and their fates are compared at the beginning of Book IV.,[3] while Amoret alone can wear the girdle Florimell has lost. Both are held captive, and the tapestries portraying Jove's metamorphoses in the House of Busyrane are an echo and reminder of the transformations which Proteus undergoes earlier in the same book in his attempts to win Florimell.

It may be that in trying to define the meaning of such myths as these one can only rob them of their power. " Symbols are the only things free enough from all bonds to speak of perfection," and to limit them to a definable meaning is to bind them. Yet one may perhaps suggest, if only as one possible meaning among the many meanings which Spenser's myths contain, that Florimell is the prototype, in the world of inanimate nature, of the steadfast womanliness of Amoret. Both are saved by truth to the nobler and more constant elements of their own being, for Amoret overcomes enslavement to physical passion by the power of chaste and enduring love, while through her love for Marinell Florimell escapes from the mutable Proteus and so finds safety and the unchanging peace at the heart of a

---

[2] As a symbol of unity in multiplicity, and of constancy in apparent change, the sea is most fully expressed in the marriage of Thames and Medway (IV., xi), where the description of the guests moves from old Ocean through the many rivers which have their source in him, to end in a superb picture of multiple unity in the Nereides, the innumerable changing waves of the sea. Sir John Davies writes similarly of rivers that " with the sea (their) course is circular." (*Orchestra*, 63)

[3] IV., i, 1.

changing world. The two may be remote from one another,
but they embody the same truth: that escape from bondage to
what is fleeting and inessential can be achieved by a steadfast
attention to eternal values, and that so we may work our own
perfection. Man and nature both, apparently bound by the
physical, subject to chance and change, have none the less their
share in lasting truth. So Florimell's world and Marinell's can
shadow the things above them, just as Cymoent's bower of
hollow waves imitates the home of the gods, being vaulted

> like to the sky
> In which the Gods do dwell eternally.   (III., iv, 43)

Contemplating their life, we may " in those weaker glories spy
Some shadows of eternity."

But it is a blind and innocent life, striving only for survival
and self-protection through avoidance of danger, and unable
to comprehend the decrees of fate and justice which work
through it. Cymoent and Proteus have only faint inklings of
the true meaning of the prophecy which Proteus himself makes.
Yet justice works even by means of that blindness, and the sea,
which is its instrument in ending the troubles of Florimell,
forms a background still to the adventures of Artegall in Book
V. Artegall himself enters the story of Florimell and Marinell
when he deals justice at their wedding in the affair of the false
Florimell, and the Book of Justice draws together some of the
themes of earlier books. The Proem is another version of the
theme which appears in so many guises in *The Faerie Queene*,
and is hinted at in Florimell's story; that of change and constancy. Mutability in the natural world is paralleled by inconstancy and a lack of proper values in man, but beyond this
instability Justice, the " most sacred vertue," lives unchanged,

> Resembling God in his imperiall might.   (V., Proem 10)

Artegall's reply to the giant in Canto II. continues the theme,
with its echoes of the Garden of Adonis and of Concord who
holds the parts of the universe together

> As their Almightie Maker first ordained.   (IV., x, 35)

Concord persists even through the hostility of the world, and

Providence works through apparent change and loss in the interests of a wider justice.

> What though the sea with waves continuall
> Doe eate the earth, it is no more at all:
> Ne is the earth the lesse, or loseth ought,
> For whatsoever from one place doth fall,
> Is with the tide unto an other brought:
> For there is nothing lost, that may be found, if sought.
>
> Likewise the earth is not augmented more,
> By all that dying into it doe fade.
> For of the earth they formed were of yore,
> How ever gay their blossome or their blade
> Doe flourish now, they into dust shall vade.
> What wrong then is it, if that when they die,
> They turne to that, whereof they first were made?
> All in the powre of their great Maker lie;
> All creatures must obey the voice of the most hie.
>
> (V., ii, 39-40)

The giant's notion of justice is presented as false not only in the case of human institutions but in relation to the whole of the created world, and it is the sea, symbol of ultimate unity and of the justice present in all things, which swallows the giant and all his works. The " mighty sea " is again the instrument of Providence in the episode of Amidas and Bracidas, for its " imperiall might " [4] is a manifestation of the power which disposes of things justly for nature and man alike.

Spenser's interlinked themes are now so well established that in Book VI. he is able to add to his symbols, but here too he writes much of nature, and of the exchanges of courtesy proper to it, for the charm of courtesy in man has its counterpart in the poetry of a pastoral world. Florimell has her place here too, for she was reared by the Graces on that same Acidalian mount [5] on which they appear to Colin, where nature is at its loveliest and most fruitful, the heightened but still truthful nature of poetry. Spenser indicates the importance of the passage by his almost reverent preparation for it; and part of its importance may lie in the impression it gives of the order and unity of things as they appear to the shaping mind of the poet. The

[4] Compare V., Proem 10.   [5] IV., v, 5.

double circle of the dancing ladies moves, to Colin's piping,
around his "countrey lasse," poetic symbol of all grace and
virtue, while the imagery suggests earlier, related themes. The
treatment of nature contrasts with that of the Bower of Bliss,
the bridal imagery of Ariadne is a reminder of the Garden of
Adonis and the Temple of Venus, and Florimell, child of the
Graces, is also part of this ceremonious world of love, poetry,
and natural grace. The passage is almost a copy in little of the
widening circles of the poem and its meaning.

But the latest and fullest of such unifying passages as these
is to be found in the fragment *Of Mutability*, a more explicit
statement of the great theme which earlier books express chiefly
by symbol and by arrangement of material. These two cantos,
and the two final stanzas, are the culmination of the poem as
it now stands, both unifying and illuminating it. Spenser's
description of Nature, and Mutability's address to her, show her
as the source—or rather as nearest to that source which man
may know—of the conceptions in other books. She embodies
Justice and Concord, she is veiled like Venus, and by her likeness to the transfigured Christ she suggests the Holiness of
Book I. Mutability, on the other hand, is Corruption,[6] sin,
or the consequences of sin as seen in our world:

> For she the face of earthly things so changed,
> That all which nature had establisht first
> In good estate, and in meet order ranged,
> She did pervert, and all their statutes burst:
> And all the worlds faire frame (which none yet durst
> Of Gods or men to alter or misguide)
> She alter'd quite, and made them all accurst
> That God had blest; and did at first provide
> In that still happy state for ever to abide.   (VII., vi, 5)

She is of mortal race, for it is this which saves her from the
anger of Jove, and it is she who

> death for life exchanged foolishlie;
> Since which, all living wights have learned to die.
>   (VII., vi, 6)

In her pride she has distorted what God had left in good order,

---

[6] C. S. Lewis, *The Allegory of Love* (Oxford, 1936), p. 354.

has broken the laws of nature, justice, and policy, and has brought death into the world. She is a composite creature, for in her beauty can be seen the charm of Florimell's world of innocent partakers in the sorrows of man, but in her too is the guilt of man himself. The story of Faunus and Molanna is a pathetic and absurd parallel to the high seriousness of Mutability's trial and its theme of the effects of sin upon the world. Through the stupid presumption of Faunus the sacred Arlo hill, once the haunt of Diana and the setting chosen for Nature's court, becomes a place of desolation.

The issue of the trial is made clear. Mutability's claim to rule over the earth is allowed, but Jove retains his sway over "Heaven's empire," and is "confirm'd in his imperiall see." Indeed, once the realm of earth is left behind, and the higher places of the Universe are approached, Mutability's arguments lose much of their force. Her struggle with Cynthia in the sphere of the moon, traditionally the border of the regions of decay, is left unresolved, and her answer to Jove's claim that the gods control time and change is hardly conclusive. She begins with a flat denial:

> What we see not, who shall us perswade?   (VII., vii, 49)

and continues with a description of the changes of the moon and the motions of the planets which Nature has no difficulty in answering. The moon may have its phases, and the spheres move, but they return again to themselves.

> They are not changed from their first estate,
> (VII., vii, 58)

for time and change are, as Jove has claimed, part of God's plan. But Nature's reply presumably deals with the whole of Mutability's case, including her claim to earth, and one may suppose that even there, where through sin and death she does now rule, the guidance of Providence is not absent. Even there things " by their change their being doe dilate," and are being led to

> that same time when no more Change shall be,
> But stedfast rest of all things, firmely stay'd
> Upon the pillours of Eternity.   (VII., viii, 2)

On earth, the calm and orderly process through which the universe works it own perfection has been disrupted by sin, and is more difficult to perceive; but heaven can make use even of the disasters which sin has brought, and will at last bring the earth " to itselfe again," resolving change and death in eternal rest.

It is the world through which all the characters of *The Faerie Queene* can be seen to move, a world in which the linked orders of created things range from the least conscious and least spiritual upwards to the ranked angels

> Singing before th' eternall majesty,
> In their trinall triplicities on hye,   (I., xii, 39)

and in which God has ordained for each creature a steady movement towards its own perfection. Even in the life of man and of the hapless creatures which share in his fall, the remnant of this joyous order may still be seen in the justice and love which Spenser shows us at work in so many spheres and embodies in myth and symbol. Even now, if he is steadfast in devotion to truth, man may experience directly some part of the glory of eternity. Red Crosse, his quest over, delights in the company of Una,

> Yet swimming in that sea of blisful joy,   (I., xii, 41)

and hears for a moment the songs of the angels themselves. All the virtues have their home in that Sabaoth, and on earth they are all—Holiness, Chastity, Temperance—made manifest by a constant attention to the unchanging truth. It is this proper movement of all the richness of created things towards the unity which produced them and works through them that the poem expresses, and by one of the fortunate chances of poetry it ends, as we have it, with the two great stanzas which sum up the Spenserian universe:

> For, all that moveth, doth in Change delight:
> But thence-forth all shall rest eternally
> With Him that is the God of Sabbaoth hight:
> O that great Sabbaoth God, grant me that Sabaoths sight.
>   (VII., viii, 2)

At the end of the poem, " the total life has suddenly displayed its source."

University College of South Wales

III

SPENSER AND IRELAND

By RAYMOND JENKINS

Ireland had a tremendous influence on the career and imagination of Edmund Spenser. This savage island was his home from 1580 till his death in 1599. As secretary and aid to the generals, Lord Arthur Grey and Sir Thomas Norris, he witnessed some of the most bloody and gruesome campaigns in English history. The poet was an eyewitness of the massacre at Smerwick, when at the orders of Lord Grey the garrison of more than six hundred Papal soldiers was ruthlessly slaughtered.

From the time of Grey's recall in 1582 till he became Clerk of the Council of Munster in 1584, Spenser apparently lived at New Abbey near Dublin. For the next five years the poet was secretary to the Presidents of the Council of Munster, Sir John and Sir Thomas Norris. Late in 1588, on Norris' military expedition against the Spanish survivors of the Armada, Spenser almost certainly beheld the immense wreckage of Spanish ships on the coasts of Connaught and Ulster. Before March 24, 1589, Spenser occupied Kilcolman and forcibly dispossessed the Anglo-Irish claimant, Lord Roche. After his visit to England with Sir Walter Raleigh to present *The Faerie Queen* to the "Most Magnificent Empress," the poet was a planter at Kilcolman. In 1595 and 1596 he wrote the *Veue of the Present State of Ireland*. In 1598 the poet was appointed Sheriff of Cork. When Tyrone sacked Kilcolman, overran Munster, and forced the English planters to take refuge in the walled port towns, Spenser was selected to carry the news of the fate of Munster to the Queen. The work of his life was shattered, and his efforts to save Ireland for the English bore too heavily upon him. He died three weeks after he delivered his message to Greenwich.

Before we consider the influence of Ireland upon Spenser's character and achievements, we should realize the miserable conditions which generally prevailed. Only in a small section

51

around Dublin, occupied by a civilized population who lived in good houses and engaged in trade, was there a consistent administration of justice. All laws, both civil and religious, which make for an ordered polity, had lapsed. Marriage rites had fallen into disuse and were openly scoffed at. Illegitimacy was common and involved no disgrace. Shane O'Neill averred that his father, who was a gentleman, never refused any child that any woman declared to be his; and Shane followed his father's example.

The oppression of the strong prevailed everywhere. As a consequence of constant warfare between rival Irish factions and of repeated military expeditions of the English to impose the Queen's authority, Ireland was generally desolate. A picture of the straits to which the Irish were reduced, after the English under Grey had quelled the Desmond rebellion, is provided in Spenser's moving account in the Veue:

" Out of everye corner of the woode and glenns they came creep-einge forth upon theire handes, for theire legges could not beare them; they looked Anatomies of death, they spake like ghostes, crying out of their graves; they did eat of the carrions, happye wheare they could find them, yea, and one another soone after, in so much as the very carcasses they spared not to scrape out of theire graves; and if they found a lott of watercresses or shamrockes theyr they flocked as to a feast for the time . . . that in short space there were none almost left . . . yett sure in all that warr, there perished not manye by the sworde, but all by the extremitie of famyne which they themselves had wrought."

Fire and famine had reduced the people to the condition of savages, for they donned the skins of beasts and lived in holes in the ground. Any district which improved was reduced either by cattle raids or by cruel exactions, known as coin and livery. Usually the English soldiers garnered what thieves and cattle raiders had failed to get, for they lived off the helpless and peaceful Irish farmers who still tried to carry on. So wretched was life in Ireland that Sir Henry Sidney, no senti-mentalist, said of the Irish: " Surely never people lived in more misery than they—such misery as in troth hardly any Christian with dry eyes can behold."

The many accidents by flood and field which Spenser underwent in Ireland awakened the imagination and hardened the sensibilities of a very sensitive poet. To a man who had witnessed the execution of Murrogh O'Brien, the gruesome Irish heads blackening on the walls of Dublin Castle, the massacre at Smerwick, and the horrible famine in Munster, there was naught on earth which could stir more deeply one's feelings of pity and fear. In the descriptions of the horrible in the *Faerie Queene*, the poet's imagination never needed to work in a vacuum. The allegory of Despair in the First Book, for instance, is the response of Spenser's imagination to that awful spectacle in Munster. The figure of Despair takes on the form and feature of a starving kerne. Not only was the poet haunted by such hollow-eyed spectres of death, but he was also struck with fear at the thought of being a similar victim. In the tenth canto, in describing the seemly obsequies due the dead, Spenser suddenly breaks forth:

Ah dearest God me graunt, I dead be not defouled.

Even in Dublin Spenser probably beheld many bloody scenes. He may have been present at a trial by combat between the leaders of the Leinster O'Connors, Teig MacGilpatrick and Connor MacCormac. The combat was, under the guise of friendship, secretly fomented by the English officials. The whole affair was carried off in true mediaeval fashion. The Lords Justices and Council and all the military solemnly surrounded the inner castle yard, and the trumpet sounded the onset. As the English wanted the fight to be gory, the contestants were allowed only sword, target, and skull cap. Connor, twice wounded in the leg and once in the eye, attempted to close. Teig, seriously wounded " tho not mortally, the more was the pity," stunned his kinsman, then cut off his head, and presented it on his sword's point to the Lords Justices, one of whom was Spenser's friend, Archbishop Loftus. The poet must have been shocked and hardened by the callous attitude of his English associates toward this constant strife. The intensity of his feelings on such occasions made him a vehement exponent of the repressive policies of Grey, for he yearned to see internecine strife blotted out from Irish history forever.

The poet's experiences would naturally exercise an unmistakable influence upon the form and substance of the *Faerie Queene*. The conflicts and adventures of his knights, in fact, are almost a transcript of the warfare of the English leaders in Ireland. Often in the *Faerie Queene* do savages rush out of the mountains and forests to attack his knights, to lay siege to a castle, or to fall upon a peaceful hamlet, robbing, despoiling, and carrying off captives for ransom. With its trackless woods and unexplored fastnesses, Ireland provided a fit theatre for the ambushes, temptations, and enchantments against which Spenser's champions of virtue must be continually on guard. It also provided the poet with countless characters who were like Sansfoy, Sansloy, and Sansjoy, Pyrocles and Cymocles. Virtually all of the Irish leaders would appear to Spenser as impersonations of intemperance or excess in some of its worst forms, especially lust and wrath. For his champions Spenser mirrored his patrons at the court of Elizabeth; for their opponents he mirrored her enemies in Ireland. Archimago reminds us of the Jesuits—Sanders and Allen, Pollente of the Earl of Desmond, and Maleger of Shane O'Neill.

The vicissitudes of Ireland, both in the council room and on the tented field, drove into Spenser's consciousness the Calvinistic conviction that the righteous life involved a bitter warfare with gigantic forces of evil. And that warfare in the *Faerie Queene* bodies forth the constant clash between the poet's idealized vision of noble human beings and his disheartening perception of the gross flaws of the actual men among whom he lived. Surrounded by repeated rebellions and tribal wars, by constant bickering and backbiting between English officials, Spenser became fully conscious of the notable differences between the ideal Platonic world which he had envisioned as a student at Cambridge and the actual world in which he lived, and moved, and worked to make a living.

This consciousness did not divert him from his youthful desire for fame or from his ambition to improve his worldly estate. With these ends before him, he led a life of indefatigable industry. Though his labors under Grey and Norris must have forced him to work intermittently on the *Faerie Queene*, he never forsook his hope of being the Prince of Poets of his time, the Virgil of the Elizabethan age. To achieve the leisure essential to this end he secured in 1589 a deputy for the clerkship in Munster. Like Shakespeare, Spenser appears to have been a hardheaded and astute man of business. He never lost sight of the fact that even a poet must live. Though he sought honor amid the dangers of a strenuous life, he did not cast aside the opportunities for acquiring a competence which came his way as secretary to Grey and Sir Thomas Norris. He accepted whatever gratuities a generous patron like Lord Grey could give him. His dealings with Lord Roche show him as persistent in maintaining his legal rights, even to the extent of using force to oust his adversary's tenants. Around 1597, after the birth of Peregrine, Spenser added considerably to his holdings in Munster. Throughout his life the poet was ambitious to establish an estate and found a family.

Now what was the effect of this ambition, considering his original poverty, upon his poetry? It may be the reason for its lack of humor and dramatic power. The wholesome geniality and ironic humor of Chaucer, that sense of the eternal comedy of life, are not characteristic of Spenser. There is little laughter and little tragedy in the *Faerie Queene*. As Jusserand says, " Spenser's heart remains quiet and the stanzas continue smooth and regular." A man who is anxious to get on cannot look patiently at the comic aspects of his fellow creatures. Amid his Irish surroundings Spenser's outlook upon humanity was especially confined. The Irish, with their intemperance and love of fighting, had few qualities which Spenser could regard with humor. This fact intensified the rigor and moral fervor of his character.

But Spenser, like most of us, was able to reconcile the conditions incident to his advancement with his idealism. By rationalizing he managed to maintain his self-respect. Like every conservative Englishman, he accepted the principle of vested rights. Only by the acceptance of dogmas regarding earthly authority, such as were implicit in the theory of the *Great Chain of Being*, could Spenser perceive any possibility for either peace or stability in Ireland. In refuting the communistic arguments of the Giant who favors a redistribution of property, Artegal resorts to the argument that inequality is part of the inscrutable workings of Providence:

> He maketh Kings to sit in sovereignty;
> He maketh subjects to their powre obay;
> He pulleth downe, he setteth vp on hy;
> He giues to this, fron that he takes away.
> For all we haue is his: what he list do, he may.

Considering the grants which Spenser accepted from Grey, one is astonished at the gusto with which he describes the destruction of the monopolist and extortioner, Pollente, and his daughter Munera, or Bribery. Yet Spenser was certainly not conscious of any inconsistency. Tho he was an artist in flattering Elizabeth, he never considered himself a flatterer. Tho he persistently looked to the main chance in Ireland, he never thought himself either grasping or ambitious. Indeed, he thoroughly despised ambitious and intriguing courtiers.

Spenser's experiences in Ireland probably made him more rigid in his political self-righteousness. Yet he did not, unlike virtually all the English officials in Ireland, believe that no good thing can come out of Nazareth. He was not blind to the malpractices and injustice of the English; nor was he the bigot that Irish critics would make him appear. In the *Veue* he admitted that many of the woes of Ireland were due to English chicanery, that most of the English governors never wanted English law to apply to the Irish, that many of the English in Ireland had become more lawless and licentious than the wild Irish. He deplores the intolerable exactions of English bands at cess, who abuse and despoil the Irish villagers, inciting them to rebellion. Nor does the poet fail to praise the Irish for their better qualities: their endurance of hunger and cold, their courage and scorn of death. He pleads that the laws should be fashioned to the manners of a people and not imposed according to a strict rule of right. He also is very practical in his suggestions for improving the conditions of the tenantry, for building of highways and fences to prevent cattle-raiding, for instruction of the Irish in religion by native converts to Protestantism.

After reading Spenser' *Veue*, one gets the impression that Spenser was about as tolerant toward the Irish as any Englishman of the 16th century, acquainted with conditions at first hand, could afford to be. Both his national prejudice and his experience in Ireland intensified his low opinion of the Irish

He looked upon most of them as a degenerate race of cattle thieves and robbers. Besides, Spenser's religious and political feelings were so strong that he was incapable of real tolerance. Neither he nor his high-minded friend, Sir Philip Sidney, could realize that their attitude toward Dutch Protestantism was, to an unprejudiced observer, the same as the Irish attitude to papistry. To Spenser, the politic Elizabeth who went from mass to service showed herself an astute angel; but Henry IV who went from service to mass showed himself a son of the devil. As Jusserand says, " All the enemies of Elizabeth are false, repulsive, and have foxes tails at their rumps." To Englishmen, Ireland was the scene of a fierce religious struggle, and the unscrupulous ferocity of both sides left its mark on the *Faerie Queene* and on Spenser. The " verray parfit gentil knight " of Chaucer too frequently in the *Faerie Queene* becomes a fierce and ruthless warrior.

The bitterness of the religious struggle then waging in Ireland intensified Spenser's devout belief in the divine authority of the monarch. Virtually all of the Irish chiefs as well as the " rascall many " were papists, and these rebellious subjects were continually exhorted by the Jesuits " to wage war to restore peace with God, and to depose the she-tyrant who would subject Christ's church to her feminine sex." This bitter antagonism of the Irish papists to Elizabeth naturally impelled Spenser, the English official and landowner, to indulge in more extravagant laudations of his sovereign. To him she was not only a divinely appointed queen but also the personified state, the only bulwark against anarchy, rebellion, and the Anti-Christ represented by the Bishop of Rome.

Together with the divine authority of the monarch, Spenser takes for granted the right of conquest; and he justifies the use of force in maintaining the dominion of the sovereign. Tho he possessed sufficient insight to admit that many laws of man, judged by the straight rule of right, were unjust, he accepted them because they safeguarded the commonwealth. One even detects a certain self-righteous exultation in Spenser's descriptions of the ruthless exploits of Talus, the iron man, who represents the strong arm of the law. The punishments exacted by Talus against the rackelly rout, which to Spenser largely

represent the degenerate Irish, are untempered by the quality
of mercy. The poet's experience in various military campaign
and in the courts of Dublin and Munster induced him to take
for granted that God intended His Englishmen to keep the
rebellious Irish kerns in subjection. Spenser regarded the in-
surrections of the Irish as capital offenses against the peace
of a divinely ordered world. And he therefore had no compunc-
tions about accepting escheated estates of the rebels. Confis-
cations were just, since the authority of the sovereign was
sanctioned by the law of Nature and of God. Besides, treason
should be made to pay its own expenses.

Spenser's career in Ireland was a considerable factor in estab-
lishing his political convictions. Was it likewise a potent force
in determining those moral convictions or virtues which he
regarded as essential to the making of a complete man: Holiness
Temperance, Chastity, Friendship, Justice, Courtesy, and Constancy? In other words, did Spenser's life in Ireland have any
influence upon his selection of those virtues which constitute the
prime themes of the *Faerie Queene*? I believe that Spenser'
conception of those virtues which were paramount in forming
a perfect character as well as of those vices which are opposed
to the development of such a type was in a measure determined
by his varied career in Ireland.

Why did Spenser choose, as the subject for the first Book
the virtue of holiness, a virtue which appears in neither Aristotl
nor the rest? Does not the answer appear to be that Spense
chose this virtue because his reflections at Cambridge, at the
Court, and in Ireland had convinced him that religion was the
foremost problem confronting the Queen? To the poet, the
eternal war of good and evil was embodied in the struggle of
Protestant England against her Catholic foes. And Ireland
possibly to a greater extent than England, was the arena where
the Red Cross Knight of Holiness, champion of the nationa
church, could exhibit his valor against the deadly foes of
the Protestant cause. For religion and politics were closely
bound together in the mind of the poet; and Irish rebellion
had impelled him to identify the Irish with supersitition an
lawlessness.

At all events, Ireland supplied much material for the poet'

imagination. The brood of Error, the seditious pamphlets and specious doctrines of the Jesuits, infected Ireland as well as Albion. In the Isle of Inisfail there were countless living enemies of the Red Cross Knight. Spenser may have intended us to think of the Pope as Archimago, of Mary Queen of Scots as Duessa, of the French king as Sans Foi, of Philip as Sans Joi, and of the Duke of Alva as Sans Loi. But for the concrete materials of his imagination, does one doubt that many embittered Irish chiefs may have furnished him with illustrations of hypocrisy, atheism, despair, and lawlessness? In describing the abode and character of Corceca, blind devotion, and of her daughter, Abessa, or superstition, Spenser had in mind the superstitious Irish who had never known truth and who were afraid of reason. The double-dealing and hypocrisy of the Irish also probably made Spenser conscious of the ease with which an ingenuous character such as the Red Cross Knight is beguiled. Constantly, in dealing with such Irish chiefs as Tirlogh Lynach O'Neill as well as the Anglo-Irish of the Pale, must Spenser have acknowledged the power of illusion, that power which leads one to take hypocrisy for guilelessness, the false faith for the true, or Duessa for Fidessa. Sophistic rhetoric, such as we find in the allegory of Despair, characterized the utterances of Sanders and his fellow-Jesuits who assured their communicants that they who did not combat heresy robbed Ireland of peace, and that all who drew the blood of Protestants were absolved by a special warrant of the Pope. In presenting a panorama of the moral dangers that beset the knight of Holiness, Spenser would naturally regard distracted and strife-torn Ireland as a better theatre than the comparatively peaceful land of England.

The next three books of the *Faerie Queene*—the Legends of Temperance, Chastity, and Friendship—might at first reading seem to have small relation to the poet's experiences in Ireland. These books deal with different aspects of love, for to Spenser love is the source of every spiritual quality. In developing the episodes of these books Spenser is intent upon showing us that these virtues exist in a state of unstable equilibrium, that they are achieved only through restraint, a militant warfare against malign forces, both within and without. And all of these baleful forces are amply illustrated in the Irish scene. The idealistic poet fervently longed for a society in which life was lived at its best, for a world in which temperance, chastity, and concord flourished. But Ireland furnished him a constant illustration of a society wherein life was lived at its worst, a land where intemperance, unchastity, and discord were the common lot.

A vice which Spenser especially condemns in these three books is sexual incontinence. Almost all of Spenser's giants or enchantresses, in fact, typify in some form either violence or lust. So common are the actual or attempted rapes in the *Faerie Queene* that Jusserand charges Spenser with lubricity. He says that the poet took pains to regale his courtly reader with a sufficient number of fine sights by the road while he was treading the pathway to the New Jerusalem. The interests of courtly readers as well as the desire to " overgo Ariosto " certainly influenced the poet. But we should not rule out the lack of civility in Ireland, for no writer's imagination works in a vacuum. Spenser declares that the lazy Irish kerns, who are fit only for the halter, are " common ravishers of women." And Sir John Davies avouches that the negligence of the civil and ecclesiastical government has filled the land with bastards. By chastity Spenser meant neither virginity nor celibacy but self-control in wedlock. In writing the Legend of *Chastitie*, perhaps he inadvertently deplored the moral degradation of the Irish.

In the fifth book, the Legend of *Justice*, probably begun just after Lord Grey's death, the poet writes an eloquent defense of Grey's administration in Ireland. The treatment of this high-minded leader, whom he thought so unjustly traduced, rankled in his soul; to vindicate Grey became one of the dominating passions of his life. He represents Artegal, on his return from his triumphs in Ireland, as met by the hags Envy and Detraction and the blare of the hundred tongues of the Blatant Beast:

> And still among most bitter wordes they spake,
> Most shameful, most vnrighteous, most vntrew,
> That they the mildest man aliue would make
> Forget his patience, and yeeld vengeaunce dew
> To her, that so false schlaunders at him threw.

Grey had died under a cloud of disgrace. Spenser thought he had been undone by backbiting, treacherous friends, who behind smiling faces wrote malicious letters in cypher to the Queen and

er Council. Spenser's elegy could do neither himself nor his
ead patron any good, but there is something admirable in the
oet's steadfast loyalty.

In the Legend of Justice, the poet exalts Grey as the ideal
overnor, the Roman type of judge who is stern in the execution
f justice. Though Spenser did not believe in extermination,
e realized the unspeakable cruelty of an easy-going tolerance
f abuses. He knew that the Irish ever interpreted clemency as
owardice and that unwarranted pardons were ever an invita-
ion to more civil wars. Spenser represents Grey's justice as a
error to the wicked and a comfort to the good. He was one
eputy who would not pardon for a gift of cattle, one who, as
ir John Davies says, " had never heard a cow speak and under-
tood not that language." Spenser exalts Grey because he was
onvinced that only the governor who would not permit " the
rish to tumble in their own sensual government " could prevent
he periodic depopulation of Ireland, a depopulation so complete
hat after fire and sword, the halter and the pestilence had done
heir work, naught but rabbits possessed the land. On his estate
t Kilcolman Spenser worked out his dreams of ideal justice and
onstancy in government, and in Grey he personified that virtue
hich is the most sacred of all the rest.

Grey would be closely associated in the poet's mind with
nother noble man, also dead ere his time, Sir Philip Sidney,
 the president of noblesse and of chevalree." Philip Sidney
ad waged a notable crusade against slander by defending the
rish administration of his father, Sir Henry Sidney. He would
herefore appeal to Spenser as an ideal Sir Calidore of the sixth
egend of *Courtesie*, the knight who was to bind the Blatant
beast in chains, for the bellowings of this beast haunt the last
wo books. Spenser's imagination, in fact, seems obsessed by
he power of envy and slander to mar the noblest life. He hated
he insidious struggle of ambitious unworthiness both at Court
nd in Ireland. And therefore, in his retreat at Kilcolman,
esirous of waging a last fight against slander, he pictures his
nightly ideal, Sir Calidore. Possibly by the time Spenser com-
osed the Legend of *Courtesie*, he had concluded that justice
ould bring no permanent peace to Ireland, unless the English
eased to defame their appointed leaders and unless they were
ourteous and kind to their Irish foes.

In the cantos of *Mutabilitie* Spenser's joy in his home seem
haunted by the fear that an Irish raid will in a moment reduc
the work of a lifetime to ruins. This consciousness makes th
poetry of these cantos so suggestive of the instability of life
The hazards of his position made it almost impossible for th
poet to reconcile his misgivings regarding the indifference o
Nature with his faith in a guiding Providence. In Ireland, a
least, it seemed that lawlessness had become omnipotent, tha
endless restlessness had triumphed over endless peace. Thoug
he avers that Mutabilitie ministers to an ultimate perfectio
wherein there shall be no change, we feel that this reconciliatio
is not clear to his heart. It is only achieved by the will; it is a
act of faith. The last stanzas of the *Faerie Queen* are therefor
the voice of a spirit utterly wearied by the vicissitudes o
Ireland; they are the cry of a spirit confronted by an awfu
mystery and unable to find relief in conventional iteratior
They are a prayer for illumination and for rest with God:

> For, all that moueth, doth in *Change* delight:
> But thence-forth all shall rest eternally
> With Him that is the God of Sabbaoth hight:
> O that great Sabbaoth God, graunt me that Sabaoths sight.

These last cantos are full of a melancholy personal significanc
for they seem inspired by the apprehension of that calamitou
uprising in which the Munster plantation was overwhelme
and the poet's fortunes ruined. Not only these cantos bu
virtually all of his great work is dominated by the shadow c
Ireland, so constant in her inconstancy. Spenser longed for th
rule of love and law, for stability and justice in this world. Bu
his career in Ireland convinced him that this yearning coul
never be satisfied. His poetry is therefore full of satiric con
plaints and idyllic visions. Since his verse invariably reflect
the changes in his worldly estate, the unrest of Ireland enlarge
the scope of his poetry and gave it a more idealistic bent. Th
instability of Erin made him conscious of the vices that b
leaguer the high-minded idealist. The constant reminders in h
environment of the baleful results of ignorance and incontinenc
deepened his moral fervor. Ireland made the poet's vision c
human life more stern; it helped to make him " grave, mora
Spenser."

Catawba College

IV

THE TRUANCY OF CALIDORE

By J. C. MAXWELL

Too little attention has been paid to Spenser's conduct of
allegorical narrative except where there are obvious difficulties
of interpretation. This has meant that in Book VI of the *Faerie
Queene*, where such difficulties are not obtrusive, a great deal
has been written on the historical interpretation of Calidore—
Sidney or Essex?—and on the Blatant Beast, but very little
about the problems Spenser faced in treating Courtesy within
the allegorical framework, and the degree of success with which
he solved them. Questions of this kind are discussed in some
of the better general books on Spenser, notably in W. L.
Renwick's *Edmund Spenser*, C. S. Lewis's *Allegory of Love*,
and W. B. C. Watkins's *Shakespeare and Spenser*, but none of
them has much space to devote to Book VI. Hence I believe
that some fairly elementary things remain to be said, and can
be said without an elaborate array of references to previous
discussions.

The normal method of Spenser in Book VI is that described
by Renwick [1] as ' typical action '—the courteous man displaying
courtesy in whatever situation he finds himself. It is in keeping
with this that Spenser should have felt impelled to introduce
variety by not having a single character in the leading role
throughout. Calidore is absent for five and a half cantos, and
courtesy is meanwhile exemplified by Calepine and Arthur.
There is an attempt to make up for a certain absence of complexity in idea and of psychological development by diversity
of incident and character, and the attempt is not entirely successful: the middle of the book, except for the capture and
rescue of Serena at the end of canto viii, is rather dull and
invertebrate. But the main tension is between the episodic and
exemplary treatment and the reiterated insistence on Calidore's
first quest.' He is offstage, unsuccessfully pursuing this quest,

[1] *Edmund Spenser*, p. 148.

for almost half the book, and in the opening cantos as well w
are several times reminded of the quest (i. 47; ii. 38; iii. 19;
There is nothing contradictory about all this: courtesy revea
itself not least in doing what comes to hand, and at the be
ginning of the last canto Spenser explicitly justifies his treatmer
of the theme:

> For all that hitherto hath long delayd
> This gentle knight, from sewing his first quest,
> Though out of course, yet hath not bene mis-sayd,
> To shew the courtesie by him profest,
> Euen vnto the lowest and the least.   (xii. 2)

None the less, we feel that either too much has been made from
time to time of the main quest or else too little comes of it i
the end. In saying this I am not thinking so much of the incor
clusiveness of Calidore's achievement as of the poeticall
rather perfunctory and anti-climactic handling of the fina
twenty stanzas of the book.

This contrast between episodic construction and insistenc
on a single specific aim becomes most acute in the Pastorell
episode and in Spenser's own comments on Calidore's behaviour
In the opening cantos Calidore has displayed courtesy in th
various situations in which he has become involved, while, a
we are reminded from time to time, not forgetting his firs
quest. In the middle of the book he is removed from ou
observation to devote himself to the quest, and we cannot hel
feeling that Spenser is glad to get rid of him for the time being
it is no longer necessary to devise for him episodes which ar
in danger of becoming repetitive, and to explain that all thi
is without prejudice to his central quest. Then he reappears i
canto ix, and the longest and finest episode of the book begins
At the opening of canto x, Spenser pauses to survey the situa
tion, and the first three stanzas must be quoted in full:

> Who now does follow the foule *Blatant Beast*,
> Whilest *Calidore* does follow that faire Mayd,
> Vnmyndfull of his vow and high beheast,
> Which by the Faery Queene was on him layd,
> That he should neuer leaue, nor be delayd
> From chacing him, till he had it attchieued?
> But now entrapt of loue, which him betrayd,
> He mindeth more, how he may be relieued
> With grace from her, whose loue his heart hath sore engrieued

That from henceforth he meanes no more to sew
  His former quest, so full of toile and paine;
  Another quest, another game in vew
  He hath, the guerdon of his loue to gaine:
  With whom he myndes for euer to remaine,
  And set his rest amongst the rusticke sort,
  Rather then hunt still after shadowes vaine
  Of courtly fauour, fed with light report
Of euery blaste, and sayling alwaies on the port.

Ne certes mote he greatly blamed be,
  From so high step to stoupe vnto so low.
  For who had tasted once (as oft did he)
  The happy peace, which there doth ouerflow,
  And prou'd the perfect pleasures, which doe grow
  Amongst poore hyndes, in hils, in woods, in dales,
  Would neuer more delight in painted show
  Of such false blisse, as there is set for stales,
T'entrap vnwary fooles in their eternall bales.

Taking the whole book in broadest outline, there would be no
particular problem, still less contradiction, in all this. Calidore
has had a quest imposed upon him. Up to now, though he has
been temporarily and justifiably distracted from it, he has
constantly borne it in mind; but now he deliberately (though
under strong temptation, which excuses him to some degree)
withdraws from it. When he finally returns to it, it is with
self-reproach:

Tho gan *Sir Calidore* him to advize
  Of his first quest, which he had long forlore,
  Asham'd to thinke, how he that enterprize,
  The which the Faery Queene had long afore
  Bequeath'd to him, forslacked had so sore.   (xii. 12).

But this is satisfactory only while we remain on the level of
the abstract notion: imposition of a quest. It is much less
satisfactory when we consider the concrete nature of courtesy
as Spenser himself presents it in the main body of the book.
C. S. Lewis offers a defence of Spenser against one possible
charge, which really brings out the way he is open to another
charge: ' The greatest mistake that can be made about this
book is to suppose that Calidore's long delay among the shepherds is a pastoral truancy of Spenser's from his moral intention.
On the contrary, the shepherd's country and Mount Acidale

in the midst of it are the core of the book, and the key to
Spenser's whole conception of Courtesy.' [2] This is true, and it
is also true that certain aspects of Calidore's courtesy are displayed in this episode more clearly than elsewhere, but this
surely makes it all the odder that the framework within which
all this occurs is, not indeed Spenser's but Calidore's, truancy
from his central quest. Spenser seems to have been conscious
of some of these difficulties. At the beginning of canto x, he
merely stresses the excuses that can be made for Calidore, but
in xii. 2, quoted earlier, he specifically cites Calidore's courtesy
among the shepherds not as a mitigation of Calidore's offence
but (anticipating Lewis) as a defence of himself against the
charge of irrelevance. And in doing so he does not distinguish
between the unavoidable distractions in cantos i-iii and the
truancy of cantos ix-xi. Too much weight cannot be put on
this, since Calidore is formally rebuked in xii. 12, but it does
suggest that Spenser was aware that the Pastorella episode was
equivocal—both a truancy and an exemplification of the central
virtue of the book—and this comes out still more strongly in
the detail of the opening of canto x, to which I now return.

There is a startling discontinuity in the second stanza. Up
to l. 4, all is clear: Calidore has neglected his first quest in order
to follow " another quest, another game," namely love. But
then we are told that he intends to remain with his love

> Rather then hunt still after shadowes vaine
> Of courtly fauour, fed with light report
> Of euery blaste, and sayling alwaies on the port.

There is perhaps no strict contradiction here with what precedes, but it takes an effort—and an effort that the reader is
given no encouragement to make—not to identify the hunt after
' shadowes vaine ' with the quest which Calidore abandons—
otherwise why is such a hunt mentioned at all? Yet on reflection such an identification for a quest imposed by Gloriana is
impossible. But we do not pause to reflect, and go on to the
excuse given in stanza 3 with the description of court life fresh
in our minds. The result is that, though Spenser professes only
to mitigate Calidore's offence by describing the pleasures of the

[2] *Allegory of Love*, p. 350.

pastoral life, we are left with the impression (which probably corresponds to Spenser's own belief) that it is not only more pleasant but also better than life at court. Under the latter term are included, and not sharply distinguished from each other, (a) pursuit of the quest of the Blatant Beast, (b) pursuit of 'shadows vaine' and 'painted show.' Spenser is in fact trying to work simultaneously with the antitheses: 'fidelity to quest *versus* life of retirement' and 'court *versus* country.' The second term in both these oppositions has the same reference; hence a tendency not to keep the first terms distinct. There is, as I have said, not a strict logical contradiction. It makes good sense to say: 'Calidore abandoned his quest in order to woo a country love, with the intention of settling down in the country and abandoning the vain delights of the court. In leaving his quest he was to blame, but there were excuses for him since country life is in itself preferable to life at court' —and on one level that is what Spenser has meant to say. But on the level on which poetry affects us as poetry he has said something much richer and more interestingly confused, as I hope I have shown.

It is only at this point that significant confusions come right to the surface, but it will be worth while to inquire into the bearing of this analysis, and of Spenser's whole conduct of his narrative in this book, on his allegorical method.

He is obviously in difficulties at the outset with the whole chivalric framework. It is not that courtesy cannot as well as any other virtue—more easily than some—be displayed in such a framework. In a sense it is *the* chivalric virtue *par excellence*, but the very ease with which it can be directly displayed is a disadvantage when it comes to displaying it allegorically, as the backbone of the whole book. Here as nowhere else in the *Faerie Queen* do we feel that the quest notion is an incumbrance. Courtesy can be shown in combat, but it is impossible to feel that Calidore's courtesy *culminates* in the allegorical fight with the Beast, as Guyon's temperance does in his destruction of the Bower of Bliss or even the Red Cross Knight's holiness (though the detail of that episode is not very well handled) in his fight with the dragon. It comes as a sad anticlimax after the rescue of Pastorella. In the Pastorella episode too, Calidore's neglect of the quest cannot be presented as an offence *against* courtesy, comparable to the backslidings of the heroes of Books I and II,[3] and Spenser reconciles himself to this, covering it up, as we have seen, with some instructive confusions. It is also notable that the Blatant Beast is opposed to courtesy not as the typical vices of the earlier books are opposed to their central virtues. Its attack symbolizes attack by discourteous persons, not the attempt of discourtesy to establish itself in the human soul. Throughout the *Faerie Queene* Spenser has used allegorical figures of both types, but in the first two books the ' allegoric core ' of the book, in Lewis's phrase,[4] has been concerned with the second type. Spenser shows his sense of the divergence of Book VI from the norm by not having the Beast attack the hero at the point in the book where such an attack by the principal enemy normally takes place. It would have no special moral significance to have Calidore, or even the secondary hero Calepine, wounded by the Beast, and Spenser brings this out by substituting as victims two peripheral characters, Serena and Timias. Even so, the handling is clumsy, and betrays a mind not fully engaged by what it is doing. Spenser always claims freedom of movement between the allegorical and the direct treatment of moral questions, but he normally manages the transition rather better than he does in VI. vi. 7, where the hermit suddenly recommends spiritual remedies for what has up to this point been on the level of narrative a purely physical injury (contrast the handling of a similar theme in I. x. 24-8).[5]

Altogether, it is hard not to feel that the typical *Faerie Queene* framework, in which a knight exemplifying a particular virtue engages in a quest that culminates in the destruction of the arch-opponent of that virtue, was little more than an encumbrance for Spenser in this book. Aristotelianism too is handled in the most perfunctory fashion. No attempt is made, for example, to invent significant action corresponding to Blan-

---

[3] I take these two books for comparison because, by common consent, they are with Book VI the most successful artistic units within the poem.

[4] *Op. cit.*, p. 353.

[5] What is wrong with this passage is not so much the transition from the allegorical to the non-allegorical as such, but the presentation of this transition as if it were the drawing of a contrast *within* the allegory.

dina's official role as the representative of the excess of the quality of which courtesy is the mean. All we have is a fossilized statement of her nature (vi. 42)[6] which has no later confirmation, for she is not even represented as a party to her husband's treachery in canto vii.

But it would be rash to see in this a permanent reaction against formal allegory. The difficulties seem to arise from the specific nature of courtesy—a spontaneous, natural virtue (cf. i. 2, ii. 2) not easily allegorized in terms of conflict and best described in terms of exemplifications which display no regular progress. One other feature of the book which has been thought to reflect a permanent change of attitude on Spenser's part may also be mentioned: the escape of the Blatant Beast. The view that this, in its contrast to the conclusions of Books I and II, indicates Spenser's disillusionment with his earlier 'idealistic scheme of life'[7] seems to me without foundation. I see no evidence that Spenser ever held any utopian views about the overthrow of evil in the world. But in the first two books, primarily spiritual and individual in their significance, the overthrow of the enemy fitted the allegorical meaning. In Book VI, in which the enemy's field of action is the world of society, there could be no such conclusion without a utopianism fundamentally at variance with Christianity.

Kings College,
Newcastle upon Tyne

[6] Osgood's statement (*Variorum, ad. loc.*) ' the full-length portrait of Blandina is worth some consideration, particularly in its verisimilitude ' is incomprehensible to me. No doubt there are and were women such as Blandina is here described to be, but Spenser does not *show* Blandina as a woman of that kind.

[7] K. M. Warren, in *Variorum,* p. 319.

V

THE THEOLOGICAL STRUCTURE OF THE *FAERIE QUEENE*, BOOK I

By Virgil K. Whitaker

Theology is a subject which the student of English literature is likely to view from afar, with indifference if not actual hostility. Yet no subject was better known, at least in its fundamentals, to Elizabethan writers. In petty school they learned to read from a primer that consisted merely of selections from the Book of Common Prayer, and they memorized the Catechism from the prayer book as well as sentences from the Scriptures. In grammar school they studied the same catechism in Latin and Greek versions and also, before 1570, the elaborate Latin catechisms of Calvin or Erasmus. After 1570 they mastered the catechism of Alexander Nowell, which has appended to it an elaborate glossary that indicates and demands an advanced knowledge of theological concepts. They seem also to have been questioned on the Thirty-Nine Articles.[1] For all but the incorrigibly irreligious, therefore, moral problems inevitably involved theological problems. Most Elizabethans thought of the connection between their daily sins and Adam's original sin as automatically as we associate turning on the light with electricity, and they were far better grounded in religious doctrine than most of us are in modern physics. This paper is primarily an attempt to show that the moral allegory of Book I of the *Faerie Queene* is theological in its structure and is based upon the arrangement of points customary in Renaissance confessionals. But I hope that it will also present further evidence of the part that fundamental theological ideas can play in the understanding of Renaissance literature.

[1] Cf. T. W. Baldwin, *William Shakspere's Petty School* (Urbana: University of Illinois Press, 1943), pp. 65-6, 89, etc.; *William Shakspere's Small Latine and Lesse Greeke* (Urbana: University of Illinois Press, 1944), I, 181, 311, etc. Alexander Nowell, *A Catechism Written in Latin*, etc. ed. G. E. Corie (Parker Society 32; Cambridge; University Press, 1853).

Since Book I, the legend of the Red Cross knight or holiness, is presented as a biography, the inference that it is a spiritual biography of the typical Christian in search of holiness readily follows and seems to have been accepted, tacitly at least, by most students of Spenser. Yet the moral allegory cannot possibly be biographical or chronological, even to the extent of being an idealized account of the struggles of the soul in quest of holiness. Red Cross's victory over Error in Canto i precedes the instruction of Fidelia in Canto x. Canto x, in turn, represents an entire progress through the disciplines of the church and the ultimate mystical experience to which a Christian might aspire; yet baptism does not appear until Red Cross falls into the Well of Life in Canto xi, from which he emerges " a new-borne knight " (xi, 34) with " baptized hands " (xi, 36). Even in the early church, in which baptism followed conversion and religious instruction, baptism would have been an indispensible preliminary for most of the experiences of Canto x; like religious instruction, it would have been needed for the complete victory over error in Canto i.

These, and many other difficulties, are solved if we assume that Book I, like Book II, is organized in terms of concepts. No points in the whole cannon of Spenser criticism are better established than that Book I and Book II show an elaborate and detailed parallelism in the sequence of episodes and that, because of their similarity, they constitute a kind of subgroup within the poem as a whole.[2] It is also well known that the temptations to which Guyon is subjected in Book II are arranged, according to the division going back to Plato, into those related to wrath and lust—the irascible in Cantos i to vi and the concupiscible in Cantos vii to xii.[3] That is, the structure of the moral allegory of Book II is based upon a scheme of classification rather than upon a biographically probable sequence of emotional experiences. It is certainly likely that Spenser would have extended the parallelism between the two books from surface episodes to fundamental structure and that the moral allegory of Book I would also be based upon a well-recognized arrangement of ideas. That probability this paper

---

[2] Cf. *The Works of Edmund Spenser: A Variorum Edition, The Faerie Queene, Book II* (Baltimore: The Johns Hopkins Press, 1933), p. 467.

[3] *Ibid.*, pp. 411, 416.

will attempt to establish as fact by showing that the moral allegory of Book I is organized according to the arrangement of Christian doctrines customary in Renaissance theological treatises and confessionals.

A few examples will establish this pattern. In Calvin's *Institutes*, for example, Book I considers the nature of God and the authority of the Scriptures and then turns to the state of man before his fall. Books II and III discuss Adam's fall, original sin, Christ's rôle as mediator, the operation of grace, justification by faith, good works, and predestination. Book IV is devoted to the church and the sacraments. The Thirty-Nine Articles of the Church of England begin with discussions of both God and Christ and define the authority of both Scriptures and creeds; from then on they parallel the *Institutes* closely: original sin, free will (and grace), justification, good works, sin after baptism, predestination; then the church, its authority and ministry, the sacraments, and miscellaneous points. A similar organization is apparent in the proceedings of the Council of Trent.[4] And Fidelia clearly begins to follow the same pattern when she instructs Red Cross " Of God, of grace, of iustice, of free will " (x, 19) .

Spenser followed roughly this same pattern as the basis of his moral allegory, omitting for obvious reasons the opening sections on God, the Bible, and Adam's state before the fall. Book I treats first of original sin, of justification, and of problems logically and traditionally associated with justification, such as the nature of sin itself, the hotly debated question of sins after justification, and predestination and election; then of the church and its functions; and finally of the sacraments. Sometimes Spenser employs ideas that were part of the theological heritage of Western Christendom; sometimes he parallels the Thirty-Nine Articles closely. Nowhere, as I have elsewhere argued at length,[5] does he present doctrines peculiar to Calvinism. This structure means, of course, that the sequence of events has no relationship to their probable occurrence in human life but may have logical meaning in the way that one point follows another in philosophic exposition.

---

[4] Cf. Virgil K. Whitaker, *The Religious Basis of Spenser's Thought* (Stanford: Stanford University Press, 1950), pp. 34-35.

[5] *Ibid.*, pp. 44-47, etc.

I certainly do not intend to imply that Book I of the *Faerie Queene* is a theological treatise or that every episode can be given a precise theological implication. For one thing, romance had to be attended to. For another, moral and historical allegory intermingle, and the claims of one must yield to the claims of the other. Spenser's method is not a rigorous and unyielding allegory but rather a compromise among conflicting elements.[6] Finally, the allegory often seems to move on more than two levels. Duessa is sometimes falsehood as the opposite of truth, sometimes false religion, sometimes Roman Catholicism, sometimes Mary Queen of Scots; sometimes, apparently, she is all of them at once. But an analysis of the moral allegory of Book I seems to show that the theological scheme of organization outlined above fits the key episodes in Book I and further illuminates them. Such an analysis will now be attempted, in so far as it is feasible in a paper of this length.

In following the traditional theological structure, Spenser would obviously skip the initial matter on God, the Bible and Creeds, and Adam's state before the fall. For him, as for his contemporaries, the logical starting point for a discussion of the path to salvation or holiness would be original sin and justification, doctrines about which centered the fundamental theological controversies of the Reformation. And it seems very likely that these are indicated by the Letter to Raleigh and Canto I. The contrast between original sin and Christian righteousness is first indicated by the transformation in Red Cross when he puts on the Christian armor, and then the process of justification is allegorized. Justification is, of course, the process by which the individual is cleared of his guilt of original sin and God's justice is satisfied for that sin by the merits of Christ's atonement upon the cross.

We first see Red Cross in the Letter to Raleigh as "a tall clownishe young man, who . . . rested him on the floore, vnfitte through his rusticity for a better place."[7] Una appeared, and Red Cross desired the adventure. Understandably reluctant,

---

[6] Cf. Edwin Greenlaw, *Studies in Spenser's Historical Allegory* (Baltimore: Johns Hopkins Press, 1932), pp. 91-96.

[7] Variorum Spenser: *The Faerie Queene, Book I* (Baltimore: Johns Hopkins Press, 1932), p. 169.

she finally agreed to accept him as a champion if he could wear the armour which she brought—that is, " the armour of a Chris-tian man specified by Saint Paul v. Ephes. . . . which being forthwith put vpon him with dewe furnitures thereunto, he seemed the goodliest man in al that company." The armor of Ephesians includes a breastplate of righteousness and a shield of faith, and these Spenser singles out for mention and places on each of them a cross, as everyone knows. " We are accounted righteous before God," says Article XI of the Thirty-Nine Arti-cles, " only for the merit of our Lord and Saviour Jesus Christ by Faith, and not for our own works or deservings "—that is, our righteousness derives from his cross, which we embrace by faith.

As the narrative begins, Red Cross and Una enter the wan-dering wood and there encounter Error, half serpent and half woman. This combination is remarkably like that which proved too much for poor Adam in the Garden of Eden and is doubt-less intended to suggest Red Cross's liability to error as a son of Adam. Red Cross enters into combat with Error, who leaps upon his shield and wraps her train about his body. " Add faith vnto your force," cries Una (i, 19). Red Cross then grips Error and she vomits forth a poisonous mess full of books and papers. He relaxes his grip, and she pours forth her " cursed spawne of serpents small " (i, 22), which " him encombred sore but could not hurt at all." Finally Red Cross strikes Error " with more than manly force " (i, 24) and cuts off her head; the little " sinlets " drink her blood and die of it; and Red Cross and Una ride on " with God to frend " (i, 28).

In calling upon Red Cross to add faith unto his force, Una was telling him to take the only initiative available under Anglican doctrine to a man in need of salvation: " that we are justified by Faith only is a most wholesome Doctrine, and very full of comfort," says Article XI. But, in recapitulating the process of justification, Spenser commits the absurdity, from the viewpoint of a spiritual biography, of showing Red Cross fully equipped with the armor of righteousness and faith before his first combat with Error—and then having Una admonish him during that combat to add faith unto his force! The poisonous vomit full of books and papers has been conjectured to be religious controversy,[8] but a more definite identification is perhaps possible. In narrating his conversion in the *Confessions*, St. Augustine distinguishes two steps. First, there came a rejection of false philosophies and an acceptance of Christian doctrine as true. But the lusts of the flesh still held him back. His conversion was complete, therefore, only after he had overcome not only the poison of false doctrine but the lusts of the flesh as well.[9] St. Thomas reflects the same tradition when he speaks of four things as necessary for justification of which two, an infusion of grace and a remission of sins, are God's gifts, and two, a free choice of God by faith and a free choice against sin, must be man's contribution.[10]

Spenser's allegory involves a somewhat illogical adaptation of these notions to Anglican teaching, which was coming to combine the Protestant doctrine of justification by faith with the traditional concepts of right reason and free will, as in Hooker. The vomit full of books and papers represents false doctrines that must be overcome by faith, which Red Cross provides on his own responsibility at the urging of Una or Truth. The " spawne of serpents small " is the lusts of the flesh that still hinder and must also be overcome; they derive their being and their nourishment from original sin, and in her death they die. But their inability to harm Red Cross, which is artistically ineffective and at first sight puzzles the reader, is in accord with the Protestant emphasis upon faith rather than works. Red Cross's " more than manly force " is due to God's grace, and he departs " well worthy . . . of that Armorie " and " with God to frend " because his guilt has been remitted and he is accompanied by God's grace. All four of St. Thomas's requirements for justification are therefore present.

But Red Cross's troubles are not over. Though the guilt of original sin, as well as of actual sins already committed, has been pardoned,[11] the proneness to sin remains. The ninth of the Thirty-Nine Articles summarizes the view universally accepted:

---

[8] *Ibid.*, p. 184.

[9] *Confessions*, VIII, v, 12.

[10] *Summa Theologica*, Ia-IIae, Q. 113, A. 6.

[11] Cf. " The Second Part of the Sermon of Salvation," *Certain Sermons or Homilies Appointed to be Read in Churches in the Time of Queen Elizabeth* (London: Society for Promoting Christian Knowledge, 1914), p. 27.

And this infection of nature doth remain, yea in them that are
regenerated; whereby the lust of the flesh . . . is not subject to the
Law of God.

Spenser goes on to show how this weakness or lust of the flesh
operates in Red Cross. In doing so, he relies upon the traditional concepts of sin derived from Augustine, elaborated by
Aquinas, and restated during Spenser's own lifetime by Richard
Hooker. He employs, in other words, the same set of ideas
which form the basis of *Macbeth*, as Professor Curry has
shown,[12] and which Milton used to explain the fall of Adam
and Eve.[13]

In this tradition, as you will recall, sin is always the false
choice of a lesser or apparent good instead of a greater or real
good. Since sin involves a false choice, it is impossible in the
presence of truth, and Red Cross must be separated from Una
before he can fall into sin, just as Guyon in Book II must be
separated from the Palmer or right reason before he can be
tempted by Phaedria or weakened almost to death by Mammon.
Man is liable to choose falsely because his reason has been
weakened and his will made inordinate by Adam's fall. The
false choice itself may have one of three internal causes: ignorance; the soliciting of the will by the appetite, which prevails
over reason; and a habit of sin built up by repeated false
choices.[14] Both Satan and other men may be external causes
of sin, not directly, but only by stimulating the imagination
or arousing the appetite, so that the internal causes of sin
operate.[15] Pride or inordinate self-love was the original cause
of sin both in Satan and in man, and pride and concupiscence, as manifested in the appetite, remain the fundamental
internal causes of sin in man.[16] Beginning with Canto ii,
Spenser shows how the lust of the flesh, taken as a type to
indicate appetite or concupiscence, separates Red Cross from
Truth and makes possible and inevitable further false judgments. Pride, the original cause of all sin, seems to serve almost
as a symbol of sin itself.

---

[12] Walter Clyde Curry, *Shakespeare's Philosophical Patterns* (Baton Rouge:
Louisiana State University Press, 1937), pp. 103-19.
[13] *Paradise Lost*, IX, 351-63, 703-09, 955-59, 997-99.
[14] *Summa Theologica*, Ia-IIae, Q. 76—Q. 78; Richard Hooker, *Laws of Ecclesiastical Polity*, I, vii.
[15] *Summa Theologica*, Ia-IIae, Q. 80, A. 2.
[16] *Summa Theologica*, Ia-IIae. Q. 77, A. 5.

As Una and Red Cross proceed, they encounter Archimago, the arch enchanter. Many of his characteristics are obviously determined by the historical allegory. But the reference to " his diuelish arts " (ii, 9) surely implies that in the moral allegory he is Satan himself, the father of lies, as the external cause of sin. If so, Spenser is showing the external forces of sin cooperating with man's internal appetite to produce sin, just as Shakespeare shows the witches, who are instruments of Satan, stimulating the evil desires already present in Macbeth.[17] If Archimago is Satan, he sets about separating Red Cross from Una quite orthodoxly by working on imagination and appetite. First, he stimulates lustful reverie in Red Cross, making

> him dreame of loues and lustfull play,
> That nigh his manly hart did melt away,
> Bathed in wanton blis and wicked ioy.   (i, 47)

> In this great passion of vnwanted lust,
> Or wanted feare of doing ought amis,
> He started vp,   (i, 49)

and encountered a false image of Una, who tried to seduce him. But Red Cross, sorely disturbed by Una's apparent falseness, " lay . . . musing at her mood " (i, 55), and by that musing Archimago was for the time being foiled. But Archimago's second assault, the spectacle of the false Una in the embraces of a lusty squire, was too much for Red Cross, whose reason succumbed to his passion. " The eye of reason was with rage yblent " (ii, 5), and he fled from Una, " pricked with wrath and fiery fierce disdain " (ii, 8). He was now separated from truth and a prey to his lower nature; " will was his guide, and griefe led him astray " (ii, 12).

The separation of Red Cross from truth is, of course, an indispensible preliminary to sin if sin involves a false choice. The following episodes seem to indicate, not a plausible sequence of experiences through which the Christian novice might go, but

---

[17] Cf. Richard Hooker: " There is not that good which concerneth us, but it hath evidence enough for itself, if Reason were diligent to search it out. Through neglect thereof, abused we are with the show of that which is not; sometimes the subtility of Satan inveigling us as it did Eve, sometimes the hastiness of our Wills preventing the more considerate advice of sound Reason . . ." *Laws of Ecclesiastical Polity*, I, vii, 7.

rather the various kinds of experiences to which a soul astray
from the truth and ruled by appetite and falsehood may be
subject. They investigate the possible consequences of that
" infection of nature " which remains even in the regenerated.
The encounter with Sans Foy suggests loss of faith. Fradubio
has made Duessa his dame and has been changed by her into a
tree, a state from which he can escape only by being bathed
in a living well (ii, 43). In other words, he has become so
habituated to sin that he has lost the reason which made him
man, reason being for Spenser, as for St. Thomas and Hooker,
the power to make value judgments or moral choice. He can
be saved only by baptism or a similar gift of God's grace, which,
as Spenser tells us later, will " guilt of sinfull crimes cleane
wash away " and " aged long decay renew " (xi, 30). The
visit of Red Cross and Duessa to the Castle of Lucifera involves
a presentation of the seven deadly sins. The meaning of Red
Cross's escape from the Castle of Pride after the Dwarf has
seen the dungeon full of captives seems to be that man, even
when deprived of the full light of truth, can escape the more
obvious sins by exercising prudence of a lower order. That this
kind of narrow and uncertain escape, with no basis in knowledge of truth, brings acute distrust and unhappiness, or Sans
Joy, is indicated by the opening stanza of Canto vi, which
compares Red Cross to a Marriner who " yet in doubt ne dares
to ioy at his foole-happie ouersight."

When Duessa overtakes Red Cross just before the combat
with Orgoglio, he has so yielded to lust for her that he has lost
his power of distinguishing right from wrong, as Spenser indicates in the opening stanza of Canto vii, which meditates on
the inability of man to distinguish falsehood from truth:

> What man so wise, what earthly wit so ware,
> As to descry the crafty cunning traine,
> By which deceipt doth maske in visour faire,
> And cast her colours dyed deepe in graine,
> To seeme like Truth, whose shape she well can faine.
>
> (vii, 1)

Does this indicate that the Orgoglio episode is merely an elaboration of the point made by the earlier encounter with Fradubio? I think, rather, that Spenser is passing on to another
theological problem.

Orgoglio's characteristics are obviously determined in larg
part by the historical allegory. It has been customary to dis
tinguish him from Duessa by calling him spiritual pride an
Duessa carnal pride, or vice versa,[18] but the text will not sup
port such a distinction. The introductory stanza of Canto viii
again an exposition of the moral allegory, plainly identifie
Arthur as the grace of God, Una as truth, and Orgoglio as Rec
Cross's " owne foolish pride " which makes him thrall to th
bonds of sin:

> Ay me, how many perils doe enfold
> The righteous man, to make him daily fall?
> Were not, that heauenly grace doth him vphold,
> And steadfast truth acquite him out of all.
> Her loue is firme, her care continuall,
> So oft as he through his owne foolish pride,
> Or weaknesse is to sinfull bands made thrall:
> Else should this *Redcrosse* knight in bands haue dyde,
> For whose deliuerance she this Prince doth thither guide.
>
> (viii, 1)

Orgoglio is therefore simply another personification of pride a
the first cause of sin and the symbol of man's liability to sin
The distinction between him and Lucifera is required by th
historical, not the moral allegory.

The explanation of this episode is probably to be found in
major theological controversy of Spenser's day. Article XVI o
the Thirty-Nine Articles will clarify the issue and show its im
portance, although it is possible that Spenser was not thinking
directly of the article. The Thirty-Nine Articles as a whole
involve a studious attempt at compromise among conflicting
religious positions, and only two of them contain outright con
demnations of Calvinist doctrines, Article XXXVII, which
speaks out clearly for royal supremacy over the church, anc
this one. Its importance is indicated by its unique intransi-
gence. After condemning the Anabaptist doctrine that any sir
after baptism is unpardonable, it continues: " After we have
received the Holy Ghost, we may depart from grace given, anc
fall into sin, and by the grace of God we may arise again, anc

---

[18] So J. E. Whitney calls him " braggart, carnal, or physical pride " but F. M
Padelford, " spiritual pride " (Variorum Spenser: *The Faerie Queene, Book I*, pp
428, 438).

amend our lives." This statement is directed against the Calvinist doctrine of perseverance in grace, the belief that " a true liuely iustifying faith, and the sanctifying spirit of God, is not extinguished nor vanisheth away in the regenerate, either finally or totally." [19] The issue focused the conflict between the humanist concept of free will, which Spenser surely accepted and wrote into the *Faerie Queene*, and the Calvinist view of man's total depravity. For if man has no part in his salvation but must depend wholly upon God's irresistible grace, any argument that he may fall after receiving grace involves the logically untenable supposition that God's grace is imperfect in its operation.

Red Cross was caught by Orgoglio when he was without the Christian armor and engaged in an act of lust. In using lust to show how man's appetite will lead him to sin, Spenser was following a tradition going back to the New Testament. Milton was later to use the same device when he first showed the effect of the fall upon Adam and Eve by making them indulge in carnal intercourse. Surely Red Cross had departed from grace given and fallen into sin. But the grace of God protected him. Of Orgoglio's first blow Spenser says:

> And were not heauenly grace, that him did blesse,
> He had been pouldred all, as thin as flowre. (vii, 12)

And Arthur, who rescued Red Cross, is identified by many signs as the grace of God. Except for him " Else should this Redcrosse knight in bands haue dyde." The death is, of course, spiritual death in the bands of sin. But, thanks to Arthur or heavenly grace, Red Cross arose again and amended his life.

Red Cross's next encounter is with Despair. The same combination of ideas is to be found in much literature of the Middle Ages and Renaissance. Witness Marlowe's handling of the theme of spiritual despair in *Faustus,* where, in his opening soliloquy, the scholar states and accepts exactly the same fallacious arguments that Despair urges upon Red Cross. But in Spenser the association of ideas once again parallels the Thirty-Nine Articles, this time " XVII. Of Predestination and

---

[19] Irish Articles No. 38, translated from Lambeth Articles No. V; in Charles Hardwick, *A History of the Articles of Religion* (London: George Bell, 1888), pp. 363, 378. This was one of the five points reaffirmed by the Synod of Dort in 1619.

Election," the penultimate article in the section on salvation. After summarizing the doctrine of predestination, Article XVII goes on to say:

As the godly consideration of Predestination, and our Election in Christ, is full of sweet, pleasant, and unspeakable comfort to godly persons. . . . So, for curious and carnal persons, lacking the Spirit of Christ, to have continually before their eyes the sentence of God's Predestination, is a most dangerous downfall, whereby the Devil doth thrust them either into desperation, or into wretchedness of most unclean living, no less perilous than desperation.

Despair's arguments turn on God's justice and his inexorable decree:

> Is not he iust, that all this doth behold
> From highest heauen, and beares an equall eye?
> Shall he thy sins vp in his knowledge fold,
> And guiltie be of thine impietie?
> Is not his law, Let euery sinner die:
> Die shall all flesh?   (ix, 47)

After snatching the knife from Red Cross's hand, Una replies by assuring Red Cross that he is one of the elect:

> In heauenly mercies hast thou not a part?
> Why shouldst thou then despeire, that chosen art?
> Where iustice growes, there grows eke greater grace,
> The which doth quench the brond of hellish smart,
> And that accurst hand-writing doth deface.   (ix, 53)

In short, Spenser has combined references to predestination and election with a portrayal of that despair which Article XVII envisions and a statement of its contrary principle that the elect should rejoice in God's mercy.

Space prevents a discussion of Una's wanderings during her separation from Red Cross. They seem, in general, to involve the plight of truth when separated from Christian protection and Christian revelation. If so, her rescue by Sir Satyrane seems to suggest that, like Dante, Spenser rejected the relatively liberal Thomistic view that virtuous pagans unacquainted with Christian revelation may find truth adequate for salvation by following the light of nature, for the Satyres hear Una's " trew sacred lore " (vi, 30) but " hauing cannot hold " her (vi, 33). Only Sir Satyrane, who is half " faerie " and has traveled "through all Faery lond" (vi, 29) "learnd her discipline of faith and veritie" (vi, 31). Spenser shared, rather, the doctrine of Article XVIII:

They also are to be had accursed that presume to say, That every man shall be saved by the Law or Sect which he professeth, so that he be diligent to frame his life according to that Law, and the light of Nature. For holy Scripture doth set out unto us only the Name of Jesus Christ, whereby men must be saved.

It seems not to have been noticed that the first stanza of Canto x not only interprets the moral allegory but also involves a major transition in the development of Book I:

> What man is he, that boasts of fleshly might,
> And vaine assurance of mortality,
> Which all so soone, as it doth come to fight,
> Against spirituall foes, yeelds by and by,
> Or from the field most cowardly doth fly?
> Ne let the man ascribe it to his skill,
> That thorough grace hath gained victory.
> If any strength we haue, it is to ill,
> But all the good is Gods, both power and eke will.
>
> (x, 1)

Red Cross has "gained victory" over spiritual foes. Yet his greatest struggle is still to come, and the very next stanza describes him as feeble, faint, weak, and raw. Something other than the final victory of life must be meant. The clue is to be found in the allusions to God's justice noticed at the end of Canto ix and in the implication of the last two lines just quoted, which enunciate the crucial point in the Protestant doctrine of justification by faith—that man's will is incapable of performing works that merit salvation, but that justification is God's free gift to those who have faith. Red Cross's victory is therefore final achievement of justification after his previous lapses. Its recognition marks the end of the section of the poem dealing with original sin, justification, and related problems, and leads to the instruction and disciplines of the church.

The parallel between the rest of Book I and the traditional theological structure needs no elaboration. Canto x, the House of Caelia, has long been recognized as depicting the instructions and spiritual disciplines of the church. It should be noted, however, that Spenser's presentation of penance led him to another and awkward repetition, this time of Red Cross's despair. Canto xi recapitulates the Christian struggle with antichrist in terms of the sacramental system, and, as Dodge demonstrated,[20] its treatment of baptism and the holy communion agrees with the Catechism's teaching that the sacraments are "an outward and visible sign of an inward and spiritual grace, and a means whereby we receive the same."

What, in conclusion, is the artistic significance of this view of the structure of Book I? First, it accounts for the repetition which is the gravest fault in the book—Lucifera and Orgoglio, the double encounter with despair, and, above all, Red Cross's combats with Error and the Dragon. On the positive side, if this paper makes its case, the very fact that the theological organization has so long been overlooked indicates the skill with which Spenser has concealed an analytical structure under the narrative of a quest, so that one of Red Cross's adventures seems to lead smoothly to another. In fact, the encounter with Orgoglio leads to the encounter with Despair far more smoothly than the proposition that man may fall and rise again precedes the treatment of predestination. From this point of view the narrative, and therefore the allegory, in Book I is far more effective than that in Book II.

Stanford University

---

[20] R. E. Neil Dodge, " The Well of Life and the Tree of Life," *Modern Philology,* VI (1908), 191-96.

VI

"IN THESE XII BOOKS SEVERALLY HANDLED AND DISCOURSED"

By W. J. B. Owen

An earlier note [1] suggested that Spenser's letter to Ralegh describes a version of *The Faerie Queene* which Spenser planned in 1590 but never wrote. This paper draws attention to some features of the letter which tend to support such an interpretation.

The argument will concern itself mainly with a single short passage of the letter, and more especially with the last sentence of it:

> But of the xii. . . . vertues [other than magnificence], I make xii. . . . knights [other than Arthur] the patrones. . . . Of which these three bookes contayn three, [Redcross, Guyon, and Britomart]. But because the beginning of the whole worke seemeth abrupte and as depending vpon other antecedents, it needs that ye know the occasion of these three knights seuerall aduentures. For the Methode of a Poet historical is not such, as of an Historiographer. For . . . a Poet thrusteth into the middest, euen where it most concerneth him, and there recoursing to the thinges forepaste, and diuining of things to come, maketh a pleasing Analysis of all. The beginning therefore of my history, if it were to be told by an Historiographer, should be the twelfth booke, which is the last, where I deuise that the Faery Queene kept her Annuall feaste xii. dayes, vppon which xii. seuerall dayes, the occasions of the xii. seuerall aduentures hapned, which being vndertaken by xii. seuerall knights, are in these xii books seuerally handled and discoursed.

---

[1] W. J. B. Owen, "A Spenser Note," *MLR*, XLIII (1948), 239-241; cf. also Janet Spens, "'The Faerie Queene': A Reply," *MLR*, XLIV (1949), 87-88, and W. J. B. Owen, "Spenser's Letter to Raleigh," *MLR*, XLV (1950), 511-512. It should have been added to my original note that the presence of the letter in the 1590 edition is all the more remarkable since Spenser had an opportunity to revise or remove it when he prepared the cancel signed Qq in the second issue of the book. It would have been almost as easy to cancel the whole gathering Pp and replace it with a new one, especially as the type was still undistributed when Qq was prepared. See Francis R. Johnson, *A Critical Bibliography of . . . Spenser* (Baltimore, 1933), pp. 15-16.

The obvious difficulty of this passage has been noted often enough: it seems to imply that " Book XII " of *The Faerie Queene* would contain both the quest of the twelfth knight and the account of the Fairy Queen's feast.[2] This is, of course, a possible scheme; Professor Draper shows how Spenser might have used it;[3] but it is hard to see that anything other than a broken-backed twelfth book would have resulted.

The difficulty is greater than the critics make it. The narration of " thinges forepaste " in a book later than the first is, of course, a defining characteristic of epic structure; but there appears to be no precedent either in practice or in theory for placing the preliminaries to an epic action in the last book.[4] More important: the structure implied by the series " xii. other vertues . . . xii. other knights . . . xii. seuerall dayes . . . xii. seuerall aduentures . . . xii. seuerall knights . . . in these xii books seuerally handled and discoursed " is not an epic structure at all. It is, on the contrary, a structure which may be defined as *repetitive*; for it involves twelve book-units each of which, after the first, repeats in essentials the narrative struc-

---

[2] See R. E. Neil Dodge in Variorum I, 334: " Yet the account given in the prefatory letter is oddly perplexing. According to one passage, the twelfth and last book is to be devoted entire to the beginnings; according to another, it would seem to be intended for the enterprise of the twelfth knight. . . . One inclines to doubt if Spenser really knew just where his plan was taking him "; J. W. Draper, " The Narrative-Technique of the *Faerie Queene*," *PMLA*, XXXIX (1924), 311, fn.: " The existence of twelve knights has troubled some critics, for, if the last book were given over to the adventures of the twelfth knight, space would seemingly be lacking for the narration of the antecedent action "; Janet Spens, *Spenser's Faerie Queene* (London, 1934), p. 28: " . . . . each [of the twelve quests is] apparently [to be] recorded in a separate book. But in the twelfth book, which is the last, is to be recorded the beginning of the whole business. . . . It looks as if Spenser were at least a book short."

[3] " Very possibly . . . Spenser would have made room for [the narration of the antecedent action] in the last two or three cantos of the final book. He would, perhaps, have brought the twelve knights together at the end of a year of adventures at a second annual feast, and there have narrated in retrospect the events that took place at the first one " (*loc. cit.*).

[4] Draper (pp. 321-322) endeavours to show that Spenser might have derived the idea from Vida and Scaliger; but he cites no evidence to show that Spenser had read either, even if it is admitted that what they say provides the authority. It is easier to accept Professor Draper's statement that " Once having determined not to describe the annual feast . . . at the beginning of his poem, Spenser may have felt that there would be no very good chance to tell of it until the end "; which is as much as to say that Spenser had no clear idea where to place the account.

ture established by the first, and makes no major contribution
towards developing the matter of its predecessor. Hence, an
account of the feast at any length (and the attention given to
the matter in the letter suggests that the account when it does
appear will be more than trivial), placed in any of the twelve
books planned as the letter describes them, would inevitably
break the back of the book concerned, and thus destroy the
symmetry of the scheme.[5] The device of entering *in medias res*
and narrating the antecedents in retrospect is, in fact, rooted
essentially in the developing structure of the epic, where what
is, logically, a retrogression is presented as part of the development; it can have no place in the repetitive structure which the
letter describes. The only solution is one which the poem could
have adopted: to use, not one major flashback, but twelve minor
ones, one to each book, the cumulative effect of which would
be more or less equivalent to the major flashbacks of Homer
and Vergil.[6] But the poem does not in fact adopt this solution:
for there is nothing, apart from the letter, to suggest that
Redcross, Artegall, and Calidore are despatched on their quests
at the feast described by Guyon in Book II;[7] all that is implied
by the brief references to the initiation of their quests is that
the Fairy Queen has at hand a stock of knights ready to under-
take chivalrous adventures. The total effect is not cumulative,
but merely repetitive;[8] and Guyon's connection with the feast
remains peculiar to himself. In sum: on the one hand, the
scheme described in the letter is self-contradictory, in that it
endeavours to impose a feature of a dynamic and developing
structure upon a static and repetitive structure; on the other
hand, an opportunity to combine a measure of development

[5] The same objection applies even more forcibly to the "epic action [scil. a full-scale battle against the Paynim king] at the end of the *Faerie Queene*, uniting the heroes of the separate quests," proposed by Miss Rathborne: see *The Meaning of Spenser's Fairyland* (New York and London, 1937), pp. 128-129, 238-239.

[6] Similarly the appearances of Arthur, according to the letter, are supposed to display individual virtues the sum of which is "magnificence"; there is no sign of this in the poem, as the critics have observed (see, for instance, Warton, in Variorum I, 319).

[7] See I. i. 3, vii. 46-47, xii. 18, xii. 41; II. ii. 43; V. i. 4, xi. 36; VI. i. 7, i. 10, x. 1, xii. 12.

[8] See the remarks of Warton on this point, and on the incompatibility of the scheme (such as it is) in the poem with the epic narration proposed in the letter (Variorum I, 319).

with the repetition is neglected by Spenser when it seems to be to his hand.

It does not follow, of course, that because the scheme is self-contradictory Spenser could not have used it; it is always to be granted that he might have had in mind some such scheme as Professor Draper suggests; and it might be argued from the comparatively numerous failures of narrative logic in the poem that Spenser was regrettably willing to accept self-contradiction when it suited him. Yet this is not the impression which the letter conveys; rather, the impression is emphatically of an author who fails to see that he contradicts himself. For the conflict of the two ideas, epic narration and restriction of each book to one knight only, implied throughout the passage under discussion, finds its most blatant statement, not in " one passage " and " another," as Dodge put it, but within the limits of a single sentence: the last of the passage cited. The impression which the letter conveys is not, then, of a broken-backed twelfth (or any other) book; it is essentially of two distinct and mutually exclusive literary structures, each as vividly, or as vaguely, conceived as the other in the poet's mind, and both struggling for description within the scope of one sentence. In short, we are observing the difficulties of a literary theorist who, for the moment and for whatever reason, is sadly muddled. To devise schemes to help the poet out of his difficulty is to assume that he himself knew what he meant. The assumption is possible but, to me at least, improbable. I infer, on the one hand, that Spenser had no idea of a suitable concluding book, or of any book containing adequate antecedents; and, on the other hand, that he had no clear notion of using the Fairy Queen's feast as a major structural element when he wrote the poem.

Both these inferences carry the further implication that the letter contains, as far as the Fairy Queen's feast is concerned, a forecast of the poem's structure which did not, and probably could not, come true. That it is a forecast is, I believe, fairly generally conceded: for, while some critics have proposed plausible schemes for the narration of " the thinges forepaste," few have argued seriously that the relevant narrative was ever written.[9] But if the account of the feast is a forecast of matter still to be written, there is no reason to suppose that details connected with it are any less matters of prediction. That is, any detail in the letter intimately connected with the notion of the Fairy Queen's feast is as likely to be a forecast of things to come, a hypothetical treatment, as the epic narration of the feast itself.

This principle is immediately relevant to the matter of the time-scheme described in the letter and that used (more or less) in the poem. It has been observed that, whereas the letter describes the first three adventures as beginning on successive days, the poem shows Guyon beginning his quest at the end of Redcross's, Britomart entering on the scene after the end of Guyon's, and so forth; and it has been concluded that Spenser had in mind twelve annual feasts (as described by Guyon in II. ii. 42) rather than the scheme described in the letter.[10] Setting aside the question discussed above, whether the poem really implies that the quests of Redcross and Scudamour began at the Fairy Queen's feast, we may clarify this supposed problem by applying the principle just stated: a time-scheme related to the Fairy Queen's feast is described in the letter; another time-scheme is at least hinted at in the poem; the two time-schemes are obviously not identical, and there is no necessary connection between them. For the one belongs essentially to the epic formula, the other is closest to the formula of repetitive structure, and the formulae are mutually exclusive. There is thus no problem: the poem uses one time-scheme, and the letter describes another which Spenser thought it possible to use; and we are not concerned to find any connection between them.

Similarly, since the episodes of "Book XII" described in the concluding paragraphs of the letter are conceived in terms

[9] J. H. Walter, "'The Faerie Queene': Alterations and Structure," *MLR*, XXXVI (1941), 52-53, suggests that Spenser included the matter in earlier versions of the present books and later removed it; obviously this cannot be proved.

[10] See the letters of A. C. Sprague and G. B. Parks in *TLS* for 27 April and 29 June 1933, pp. 295, 447. Both are concerned to reconcile the time-notes (of the 1596 text) with the letter, which is, I believe, impossible. The 1596 text can, however, be accommodated to a scheme of successive annual adventures better than Mr. Parks admits. The uncorrected time-notes of the 1590 text are merely chaotic; if these are ignored, the rest of the text fits into a scheme of successive annual adventures rather than the scheme of the letter.

of the epic formula, and since Books I-III conform rather to the repetitive structure than to the epic, it is clear that no inevitable connection between the episodes and the present books need be expected; and indeed none is convincingly made. It is true that, if we think in terms of the arithmetical sum, as it were, of narrative elements, the account in the letter of the antecedents of Book I does not disagree with the present Book I, because the book's account of the inception of the quest is expressed in the simplest terms, and is thus susceptible to supplementation by the episode described in the letter. The only relevant passages are i. 1 (line 5), i. 3, and vii. 46-47, and none of them mentions the feast. Yet, since we are dealing with a narrative poem, not arithmetic, the *ordonnance* of the narrative elements demands consideration. From this point of view, it is to be observed that, of the passages just cited, the first (cryptically)[11] and the third hint at a *Libeaus Desconus* story, and that the point of such a story is spoiled if its antecedents are not fully expressed in their chronological place;[12] once the knight has proved himself, we are not very interested in learning that his knightly qualities were once in doubt. For what this motif is worth in Spenser's hands, there is enough of it in the present Book I, and as Book I tells the story, it is hardly recognisable as a version of *Libeaus Desconus* at all.[13] That is, the three passages just cited provide about as much in the way of epic narration as can be tolerated in a version of *Libeaus Desconus* told in the epic manner. Thus the scheme in the letter looks forward to a hypothetical epic narration which would force upon the present satisfactory structure of Book I a narrative motif both unnecessary and undesirable: unnecessary, since it is already stated in Book I as fully as the nature of the case permits; and undesirable, since it would fully and specifically define the sum of the narrative elements as just such a story as is spoiled by epic narration. This paradox

[11] And hence agreeably to my earlier suggestion (*MLR*, XLIII, 240) that Book I was revised in the direction of the letter: this line must have been written with a *Libeaus Desconus* story in mind. But the amount of revision need not have been large, since the letter supplements, rather than describes, Book I.

[12] As Mrs. Bennett rightly comments: see *The Evolution of " The Faerie Queene "* (Chicago, 1942), p. 31.

[13] Most of the significant parallels are between *Libeaus Desconus* and the letter, not between *Libeaus Desconus* and the poem (Variorum I, 392-393).

echoes the conflict of poetic structures which was discussed above.

The letter positively conflicts with the present Book II since the book is not susceptible to supplementation by the episode of the Palmer described in the letter. In fact, like Book I, Book II contains, within the limits of its own minor epic structure, a self-consistent and sufficient account of its own antecedents, which assists in defining the book as a unit of a repetitive, and not of a larger epic, structure.

The letter seems to propose a supplementation in " Book XII " of the story of Scudamour, since Book III does not tell us how Scudamour came to set out on his quest; [14] and if this supplementation implies (as is sometimes supposed) the raising of Scudamour's status to that of the real hero of Book III, conflict is introduced with an earlier passage in the letter and with the present Book III.

The connection of the offending matter, not with the poem as we have it, but with the forecast version which was to use the Fairy Queen's feast distributed over twelve consecutive days, is plain in the opening formulae " The second day " and " The third day." The books whose antecedents are here described, then, are as hypothetical as is the proposed epic narration of the Fairy Queen's feast. That there are features in common between these hypothetical books and the books we have is not immediately relevant : the common features (which include, it is to be supposed, most or all of the present Book I) imply only that Spenser proposed to retain them in a newly shaped version of the poem.

According to the arguments of this paper, then, Spenser in January 1590 intended to recast Books I-III in a shape which could be supplemented by such a final book as the letter describes. This intention was not fulfilled: in 1590, as I have suggested elsewhere, because he did not find time in the haste of printing, proof-reading, and the like; in 1596, I should suppose, for any of the reasons which authors find for not attempting a major revision of unsatisfactory work, especially when it has been given the publicity and permanence of print: lack of

---

[14] The drift of the story can, of course, be seen from III. xi. 9 ff. and IV. i. 1 ff., but the effect is quite different from the quasi-Vergilian narrations of I. vii. 46-47 and II. ii. 40-44.

time, of energy, or of inclination. We do not know enough about Spenser's day-to-day existence, his habits of thinking and writing, to produce a more satisfactory explanation than this; but *Amoretti* XXXIII and LXXX suggest that between 1590 and 1596 he found burdensome whatever work he did on the poem.[15] The structure described in the letter is in any case self-contradictory, and Spenser may have been aware of it by 1596 as he was evidently not awart of it in 1590. The letter remains a curiosity of criticism, all but irrelevant to the work it purports to describe.

University College of North Wales

---

[15] If " the rest " of *Amoretti* XXXIII refers to Books I-III, as is usually supposed, is " the rest but rudely writ " a confession to Bryskett of the unrevised state of these books?

VII

THE DEGRADATION OF THE RED CROSS KNIGHT

By KERBY NEILL

The structure of Book I of the *Faerie Queene* is determined by the separation of the Red Cross Knight from Una and his subsequent alliance with Duessa, but these incidents have been so little studied in themselves that neither their motivation nor their allied moral lesson have been understood. This, in turn, has obscured the excellence of Spenser's narrative structure as well as the vigor of his moral teaching. Much of this failure has been due to the inadequacies of the studies of his relations to his religious milieu, but fortunately the broad outline of his theological position has been made clear by the recent monograph of Professor Virgil Whitaker, *The Religious Basis of Spenser's Thought*,[1] and the impact of the contemporary religious literature on Book I has been ably demonstrated in Mother Mary Robert Falls, O. S. U., *Spenser's Legend of Redcrosse in Relation to the Elizabethan Religious Milieu*.[2] The crux of the problem lies in the extent to which the Red Cross Knight is to be blamed for deserting Una and succumbing to the wiles of Duessa because in these two incidents character motivation and moral lesson join in determining the subsequent structure of the book, and Mother M. Robert has placed them correctly in the tradition of the warfaring Christian who could neither expect nor give quarter in his unceasing struggle against the enemy.

Traditional Spenser scholarship, unfortunately, has shown a strong tendency to excuse the Red Cross Knight at this point. This is well illustrated from a sampling of relatively modern and outstanding criticism. To B. E. C. Davis the Knight is a " blameless fool " who is duped because of his inexperience and crudity. His difficulties are " occasioned through his ignorance

---

[1] Stanford Univ. Publ., Univ. Ser., Lang. and Lit., VII, No. 3 (Stanford, 1950).
[2] Catholic Univ. diss., published on microcards (The Catholic Univ. Press, Washington, D. C., 1951).

and indiscretion." [3] H. S. V. Jones goes a step further and
says that he lacks prudence, that he is deficient in his critical
faculty, that he becomes the " Knight of Credulity," and that
his judgment on Una's "seeming misconduct in the hermitage " is " harsh and hasty "; [4] but on the whole he lays very
little stress on these incidents. Padelford comes much closer
to the basic issue when he notes that the knight was deceived
because " he trusted to his emotions rather than his reason,"
but he is led off the track by the earlier criticism of Whitney
and continues that " the reason for his ignorance and credulity "
is that he has only beheld Truth " darkly veiled." His chivalric
desire to succor a lady in distress brings him under the spell of
Duessa, " betrayed by his own naïve sincerity." [5] Professor
Osgood, who has done much to humanize the story at the literal
level, considers that Archimago " imposes upon the self-assured
young person with pathetic ease." He notes the realistic touches
of the narrative: " First, in a fit of righteous indignation, and
with something of the absolute downrighteness of youth, his
eye of reason is with rage yblent." Duessa " appeals to his
warm but unseasoned heart " and " soon they are engrossed
in a flirtation, which for him is innocent and most consoling "
(*Var.*, I. 442-443). Professor Bradner's recent general intro-
duction to Spenser [6] leaves the problem where he found it.

Against this intrenched position, I should like to add to the
evidence of Professor Whitaker and Mother M. Robert a summary of the material found in the text itself and to show the
relation of this to the moral interpretations placed upon similar
incidents in Spenser's major source within the genre, the
Orlando Furioso, and finally to fill in the background of witchcraft as a frame of reference for the story at its literal level.

From the text itself it should be clear that what really leads
the Red Cross Knight to separate himself from Truth and
attach himself to Falsehood is the illusion of the senses; that is,
passion, working through the senses, overthrows reason and fills

[3] *Edmund Spenser* (Cambridge, 1933), p. 90.

[4] (New York, 1930), pp. 157 and 155.

[5] *The Works of Edmund Spenser, Variorum Edition* (The Johns Hopkins Press,
Balt., 1932), I, 434-435. All quotations from the text are from this edition, here-
after cited as *Var.*

[6] *Edmund Spenser and the Faerie Queene* (Univ. of Chicago Press, 1948), pp.
108-109.

the mind with illusions. This world of illusion is the world of both falsehood and sin. The good warfaring christian is responsible for keeping his reason clear and in command, and God gives him sufficient grace to do so. This is of course, the theme of Book II, but it is also basic to Spenser's thought and functions throughout Book I.[7] What Spenser does is show the *gradual process* by which a man who has allowed his reason to be obscured by passion falls deeper and deeper into sin until it is impossible for him to escape without some extraordinary grace from above. Prince Arthur is that grace, but the Red Cross Knight has been so weakened morally by living in habitual sin that he can only be restored to righteousness by the spiritual exercises of the House of Holiness. As the spiritual guides of his century, and, indeed, of every century, have pointed out, the moral life depends on catching temptation in the beginning when it may be easily overthrown. At the hermitage of Archimago the agents of the devil get the opening wedge in the door of the knight's spiritual life, and his subsequent downfall is a logical exploitation of his original weakness. The importance, then, of understanding this original weakness is hard to overestimate.

The comments on the episodes which Spenser himself makes as narrator direct us to such an interpretation of these incidents. The lustful dream about Una, which will be discussed below in relation to witchcraft, is foreign to his chaste habits of thought. She is one " whom he waking euermore did weene, / To be the chastest flowre " (I. i. 48). The passion which it produces is " vnwonted " and unites with his " wonted feare of doing aught amis " (I. i. 49) to wake him up. At this point he is faced with the false Una, an illusion of the sense, who is so cunningly made " that weaker sence it could haue rauished quight " (I. i. 45). He is outraged by her behavior " But hasty heat tempring with sufferance wise," he waits " to proue his sence " (I. i. 50). His final reaction to her overtures is one of doubt, a doubt which is the result of his own goodness:

> Her doubtfull words made that redoubted knight
> Suspect her truth; yet since no'vntruth he knew,
> Her fawning loue with foule disdainefull spight
> He would not shend. (I. i. 53)

---

[7] See Whitaker, p. 58 and passim; Mother Robert Falls, p. 97.

When she leaves him he remains deeply suspicious, "Long after lay he musing at her mood,/ Much grieu'd to thinke that gentle Dame so light" (I. i. 55), but, since both the dream and the apparition report their failures to Archimago, who rages in frustration, it is clear that the Red Cross Knight has not fallen into sin because he has kept his passions under the control of his reason. When Archimago shows him the apparition of Una in the embrace of a squire, however, his reaction is sinful. At once " he burnt with gealous fire,/ The eye of reason was with rage yblent " (I. ii. 5). He is restrained by Archimago from killing the false pair, which, incidentally, would probably have destroyed the magic illusion, and he returns to his bed to eat his heart and " wast his inward gall with deepe despight " (I. i. 6). In brief, at this point he has entered into a state of sin; lust, anger, and even despair (" Yrksome of life," I. ii. 6) have entered his soul, and they have set up such perturbations that he is no longer under the rule of reason but as he rides off, " Will was his guide, and grief led him astray " (I. ii. 12).[8]

The moral of this literal story is closely related to the allegory which it carries. Literally the knight has allowed his reason to be clouded by passion so that he believes a great fraud about his lady's virtue. Allegorically, the devil through his agents has produced illusions of the senses which separate the mind from Truth (Una). This is a commonplace in the literature of the time.

His next step downward is to enter into a sensual rather than a virtuous relationship with a lady. Although the consummation of the knight's seduction by Duessa is portrayed in Canto vii, the nature of the relation between them is indicated at their first meeting and is the natural result of his allowing passion rather than reason to control him. After the defeat of Sans Foy, Duessa tells the Red Cross Knight a long story about her virgin widowhood, but he is interested more in the lady than in her distress, and where pity should have reigned, lust predominates:

> He in *great passion* all this while did dwell,
> More busying his *quicke eyes*, her face to view,
> Then his dull eares, to heare what she did tell.
>
> (I. ii. 26. Italics mine)

---

[8] See Whitaker, pp. 40-41.

The lust of the eyes was the first rung in the ladder of lechery, and Spenser shows the full contemporary awareness of it.[9] It is only a matter of degree which distinguishes the behavior of the Red Cross Knight from that of the roughhouse Sans Loy who snatches off Una's veil "to feed his fyrie lustfull eye" (I. vi. 4). Corflambo, whose name is sufficient indication of the allegory, conquers those who "on him lookt without good heed" (IV. viii. 39), "By casting secret flakes of lustfull fire/ From his false eyes, into their harts and parts entire" (IV. viii. 48). The first of the troops of Maleger in Book II attack the bulwark of Sight of the Castle of Alma (II. xi. 8-9), and in the diseased sensuality of Cymocles lurking in the bushes (II. v. 34), whom C. S. Lewis had called a peeping Tom, the lust of the eyes is shown as an end in itself. With the Red Cross night, however, it is the means by which he feeds the passion within him which keeps the eye of reason "yblent" so that he does not recognize Duessa's true character even after the warning by Fra Dubio. Sensuality has produced a certain blindness of mind,[10] and Duessa sees to it that the reason does not have time to probe the story of Fra Dubio when, by the time-honored device of fainting, she clouds his mind with a new wave of passion.

Spenser's less ideal knights suffer from the same trouble. Blandamour looks at the imitation beauty of the false Florimel, and it "prickt his wanton mind/ With sting of lust, that reasons eye bid blind" (IV. ii.5). Paridell enviously gazes on Blandamour and the false Florimel together, "So blind is lust, false colors to descry" (IV. ii. 11). Fra Dubio himself considers Duessa beautiful only in his "falsed fancy" (I. ii. 30); when the eye of reason is clear, Duessa appears as she truly is, not as

[9] Allan Gilbert, "The Ladder of Lechery, *The Faerie Queene* III, i, 45," *MLN*, LVI (1941), 588-594. This is a medieval and Renaissance commonplace, and warnings against rashly gazing at women range all the way from the distinguished member of the Brethren of the Common Life who always kept his eyes shut when talking to a woman (A. Hyma, *The Youth of Erasmus*, Univ. of Mich. Publ. in Hist. and Polit. Science, X, Ann Arbor, 1931, p. 93) to Spenser's sceptic contemporary, Reginald Scot, who wrote (*The Discovery of Witchcraft*, ed. Summers, London, 1928, p. 172): "The vertue conteined within the bodie of an harlot, or rather the venome proceeding out of the same maie be beheld with great admiration. For hir eie infecteth, entiseth, and (if I mai so saie) bewitcheth them manie times, which thinke themselves well armed against such maner of people."

[10] Mother Robert Falls, p. 95.

an illusion of the senses, and both Fra Dubio and later the Red
Cross Knight are horrified at the reality of falsehood.

Spenser has portrayed with considerable subtlety the entrance
of the Red Cross Knight into the life of sin. He has allowed
passion, a mixture of anger and sensual jealousy, to cloud his
reason to the extent that he believes a great fraud about his
lady's virtue, and through his roving eyes, sensually delighting
in the false beauty of a harlot, he has attached himself to
Duessa, who glibly protests too much about her respectability.
From the chivalric point of view, he has been guilty of emotional fickleness; he has doubted his own lady too easily and
transferred his allegiance to a false one too lightly. Spenser
makes this explicit at the opening of Canto iv (the italics are
mine):

> Young knight, what euer that doest armes professe,
>   And through long labours huntest after fame,
>   *Beware of fraud, beware of ficklenesse,*
>   In choice, and change of thy deare loued Dame,
>   Least thou of her *beleeue too lightly* blame,
>   And *rash misweening* doe thy hart remoue:
>   For vnto knight *there is no greater shame,*
>   Then *lightnesse* and *inconstancie* in loue;
> That doth *this Redcrosse knights ensample plainly proue.*
>
> Who after that he has faire Vna lorne,
>   Through *light misdeeming* of her loyaltie,
>   And false *Duessa* in her sted had borne. . . .

When Spenser turns to a simple allegory of the evil of inconstancy in love, in the Castle of Malecasta in Book III, he rein-
troduces the Red Cross Knight as the victim who is saved by
Britomart, the knight of Chastity. Here again the first of the
knights of Malecasta is Gardante (III. i. 45).

These examples should be sufficient to show how much the
traditional teaching on the operation of the lust of the eyes
permeates the *Faerie Queene*, and how in the portrayal of the
Red Cross Knight Spenser shows the way it can lead a young
man into the life of sin. The motivation of Red Cross, then,
becomes clear, and with it his moral responsibility. The incident is subtly handled, but the knight's final capture by Orgoglio immediately after the completion of his seduction by
Duessa follows very logically from his initial sin in the hermi-

tage of Archimago. It is there that he enters into the sinful world of illusion produced by passion and separates himself from the world of truth to which he had access by his reason. As Professors Whitaker and Woodhouse and Mother Robert Falls [11] have well stressed, fallen man can only keep his passions under the control of reason with the help of grace, but the Red Cross Knight had that gift from the beginning with the armor of a Christian man, and only after he has become imprisoned by sin in the Castle of Orgoglio must he be saved by an act of extraordinary grace found in the person of Prince Arthur.

Although it would be naïve to look for specific sources for such universal moral concepts as the rule of reason over passion or fallen humanity's need for the assistance of God's grace, yet it may well be asked how much such concepts should be considered as a part of the conscious structure of a literary work. An answer may be found in the contemporary commentary which became attached to Spenser's most popular model within the genre, the *Orlando Furioso*. Between 1561, when Spenser may have entered the Merchant Taylor's School, and 1590, when the first part of the *Faerie Queene* was published, over sixty editions of the *Orlando Furioso* appeared. Since over eighty editions had been published earlier,[12] it is not surprising that in the eyes of the young poet such a work appeared the road to success, or that with a grandiose Renaissance spirit he set out to overgo it. Most of these editions from 1543 on, however, had " allegories " incorporated in them, a term which generally meant a moral interpretation. The significant thing is that by Spenser's time the *Orlando Furioso* had become a serious ethical treatise, and from the evidence of the editions available to him, it would seem most probable that this was what Spenser set out to imitate.

It is unfortunate that the influence of Ariosto on Book I of the *Faerie Queene* has been obscured because the major study of the subject by Miss McMurphy [13] has laid the emphasis else-

[11] Whitaker, pp. 41-43; A. S. P. Woodhouse, "Nature and Grace in the *Faerie Queene*," *ELH*, XVI (1949), 202; Mother Robert Falls, pp. 100-102.

[12] G. Agnelli e G. Ravegnani, *Annali delle edizione Ariostes* (Bologna, 1933), I.

[13] *Spenser's Use of Ariosto for Allegory*, Univ. of Wash. Publ. Lang. and Lit., II (Univ. of Wash. Press, Seattle, 1924). See also J. W. Bennett, *The Evolution of the Faerie Queene* (Univ. of Chicago Press [1942]), p. 116.

where. Particularly unfortunate is her failure to see the major
relation between the Ruggiero-Alcina and the Red Cross-
Duessa episodes. In both we have a knight who is led into
sensuality by the forged beauty of a witch; in both he is
warned by a previous lover of the witch who has been turned
into a tree; in both the return to reason is brought about
through an outside agent; and in both when the mind is
unswayed by the illusions of the uncontrolled senses, it perceives the ugliness of the witch. The interpretations put on
these incidents in the commentary on Ariosto bring the material even closer to the moral lessons found in the similar incidents in the *Faerie Queene*.

The contemporary attitude towards one who succumbs to
illusions is well represented by the interpretation of Book XII
of the *Orlando Furioso*. Melissa has warned Bradamante that
the enchanter Atlante has a trick of showing his victims an
apparition of the one they love best in some state of dire distress. She warns her to slay the likeness of Ruggiero when it
appears in order to catch Atlante in his own trap, but when
the likeness does appear in chains and begs for succor, Bradamante's heart fails her, and she follows it into the enchanted
palace. In Harington's translation (3rd edition, London, 1634)
the notes explain:

[This] signifies by allegory, that a Christian having received ghostly
counsell for the health of his soule, and is instructed in true beliefe,
yet after, when the worlds and his own grosse sense represents unto
him some contrary imaginations, he thinks *Melissa* (that is, the
preacher or instructor) doth but abuse him, and tell him a tale of
Robinhood, and so they are carried into the devils pallace, where
they find nothing but shadows and illusions. (P. 101.)

So, too, the Red Cross Knight separates himself from Truth
after allowing his passions to be aroused by the deceptions of
the gross sense, and from then on he moves in the world of illusion, a world of Duessa and the devil's palace of Lucifera.

This theme is fairly constant in the commentary on the
Ruggiero-Alcina episode. In one of the most popular editions
of the period, Ruscelli (Venice, 1565) [14] gives a similar interpretation to Canto 12:

[14] The Italian editions of Ariosto cited here went through numerous printings.
I have used the Folger Library copies.

Ci propone un come perpetuo laberinto d'intrichi, nelle cose da noi
molto desiderate. Et come gli sfrenati desiderij ci appannan la uista
dell'intelleto, & non ci lasciano riconoscere nè amici, nè altri, & ci
fanno quasi non mirare in altro, nè hauere il pensiero, se non à
ritrouare, & conseguir las cosa che noi bramiano. (P. 113.)

Horologgio (Venice, 1566) echoes this interpretation in his
comments on the same canto. These inc¡dents are shown us,
he says,

perche ueggiamo con l'occhio del giudicio, quanto siamo facili a
lasciarci ridurre da gli nostri ciechi desideri, a seguire la falsa
sembiãza di quella cosa, che più ci diletta; di modo che rinchiusi
poi nel luogo incantato andiamo sempre errando, e ricercando il
falso, che ci hà ingannati; ne lo possiamo giamai godere a uoglia
nostra.   (Fol. 53)

This formula by which the eye of reason became " yblent " is
fairly constant. The shield of Atlante is merely another example of how the dazzled senses blinded the eye of reason.
Horologgio's interpretation is typical:

Lo splendore dello Scudo incantato di Atlante, non è altro, che'l
raggio della bellezza mortale, che percotendoci l'intelletto, e la
ragione, l'inuaghisce, e l'incanta di maniera che deuiandolo dalla
uera & eterna bellezza, il rende prigionero dello irregolato desiderio
delle delicie del mondo.   (Fol. 8)

The commentary of Valvassore (Vencie, 1567) echoes these
thoughts: " Nello splendido scudo, col qualo Atlante abbaglia
la uista de gli huomini, s'esprime, come gli occhi della mente
siano offuscati dal consupiscibile appetito, inuaghendosi di bellezze mortali " (p. 12) . Spenser's " eye of reason " is a commonplace term in these texts.

When we come to the story of Astolfo, which Spenser uses as
his direct source for the Fra Dubio episode, the commentary is
only a particularization of the same general theory. The transformation of Alcina's lovers into trees, animals, etc., etc., is
merely an allegory of the loss of reason. It is briefly stated in
one of the most popular texts (Venice 1548) : " In questo sesto
canto per Astolpho trasformato in pianta, comprendesi l'huomo
dato in preda de lo appetito perdere i sentimenti humani "
(Fol. 24ᵛ) . With slight variety the commentary of Horologgio
explains:

Alcina, che trasforma gl'innamorati suoi in fieri, in arbori, in pianti,
e in fonti; ci mostra, che la uoluttà quando diuiena per uiltà nostra,
tiranna di noi medesimi, ci risolue, quando in pensieri ueramente
bestiali; quando in legno, in piante, e in acqua, priuandoci delle
operationi, che ci fanno conoscere per huomini.   (Fol. 24ᵛ)

The transformation of the body to make it conform to the
brutalized soul is the commonplace Renaissance interpretation
of the Circe myth, as has already been pointed out in relation
to Acrasia.[15] The return to one's original shape is an allegory
of the return to the life of reason. Melissa frees Ruggiero from
the illusions of his senses (the enchantment of Alcina) and sets
Astolfo and the others free also with her magic ring of reason.
This allegory is clear in the text itself where Ariosto makes his
own wry application to the frauds perpetrated by the beauti-
cians of his own day. He suggests that the feminine and cos-
metic illusion may be revealed by reason. In the loose translation by Harington it runs, " But he that had the rule and ring
of reason,/ Should soone their frauds, their crafts and guiles
discover " (p. 57).

The commentators, however, elaborated on this incident in
more serious moral terms. In the *Bellezze del Furioso* (Venice,
1574) Toscanella writes, " Melissa, che con l'anello fá conoscere
à Ruggiero la brutezza d'Alcina, & i suoi incanti; significa la
ragione, che con lo aiuto del discorso fá conoscere all'huomo la
brutezza della concupiscenza, & i suoi effeti cattivi, che sono,
come incanti " (p. 78). In his commentary Horologgio also
stresses how reason may be awakened with outside help:

L'anello posto da Melissa nel dito di Ruggiero per liberarlo da
gl'incanti d'Alcina, è la ragione risuegliata dall'altrui prudentia, con
la quale uegniamo poi in cognitione di noi medesimi, con la qual
cognitione possiam uedere anchora quanto sia sozzo, e biasmeuole
quel uitio, che prima ci pareua bello e piaceuole.   (Fol. 29)

The two steps in this awakening should be noted: first he gains
a self-knowledge that reveals his recreancy and then he sees his
seductress in her true light as an ugly witch. Fra Dubio, the
Red Cross Knight, and Ruggiero all have this experience. The
general idea, however, was common enough. In the sixteenth

---

¹⁵ M. Y. Hughes, " Spenser's Acrasia and the Circe of the Renaissance," *JHI*, IV
(1943), 381-399.

book of *Jerusalem Delivered*, Rinaldo is freed from Armida when his awakened reason enables him to see his own recreancy even though Armida loses none of her outward beauty. In Jean de Cartigny's *The Wandering Knight*, where the allegory is woodenly literal, the enchanted castle disappears when reason awakens, but he is still mired down until grace rescues him.[16]

Although Spenser illustrates this use of outside help to awaken reason or to keep it in command through the dwarf at the palace of Lucifera and through the Palmer in the story of Guyon, he carries it a step further into the theological sphere when he makes Arthur come to the rescue of the Red Cross Knight as a symbol of heavenly grace. This, again, was commonplace enough in medieval allegory, but in the commentary of Valvassore, Melissa is interpreted as showing the dependence of reason on grace: " Per l'anello post da Melissa nel dito di Ruggiero incantato, onde ne ricupera il conoscimento: s'inferisce che la perduta ragione ci è restituita per gratia, & non per accorgimento humano " (p. 62). Again, he sees the return of the other lovers of Alcina to their original forms by Melissa, " demostrano come remouendosi l'anime da uitio, per diuina gratia risorge la ragione " (p. 71). Neither his reason alone, which seems to have operated already on his experience, nor the Red Cross Knight can bring back to Fra Dubio his original shape, but he and Fraelissa await God's grace to restore them. " We may not chaunge . . . this euil plight,/ Till we be bathed in a liuing well " (I. ii. 43). Once he has finally given himself to Duessa at the fountain, the Red Cross Knight can no longer save himself, and he, too, awaits God's grace symbolized by Prince Arthur.[17] He reunites him to Truth (Una) and together

---

[16] Tr. W. Goodyear (London, 1581), pp. 51-52. Note also the commonplace interpretation of sinful pleasure: " Thou hast been wickedly inchaunted, thus to find evil in steede of good." For a rather irresponsible collection of parallels in this work to the *Faerie Queene*, see Dorothy Atkinson, " *The Wandering Knight*, the Red Cross Knight, and 'Miles Dei,'" *HLQ*, VII (1944), 109-134.

[17] See Whitaker, pp. 42-46. As Professor Whitaker recognizes, the Red Cross Knight was in grace at the beginning of the story, and his subsequent adventures are the story of his fall, but at the same time the question of the special rescue by Arthur of both Red Cross and in Book II of Guyon suggests the operation of grace irrespective of any cooperative response on the part of the recipient. This may be an attempt to show man's utter dependence and God's great benevolence, since Spenser does not appear to hold the deterministic views of Calvin. The question is too involved to be settled here.

they open again for him the eyes of the mind and he sees Duessa in her true form. In the stripping of Duessa, Spenser has enlarged somewhat on the revelation of the true ugliness of Alcina, but the total impact of Spenser's text on the reader is probably no greater than the total impact of text plus commentary in the contemporary editions of the *Orlando Furioso*.

The modern tendency to excuse the Red Cross Knight for falling into the trap of sensuality and worldly delights finds little historical backing in Ariosto. The *Faerie Queene* and the edited *Orlando Furioso* are both serious ethical treatises which reflect the current teachings of their day. Professor Whitaker and Mother Robert Falls have shown how closely Spenser echoes the theological works and sermons and homilies of his time. What might be called Ariosto moralized, that is, the interpretations of his text, shows how much of this material was read into his major literary model,[18] and in the incidents under discussion even the particularization of this material becomes evident in those incidents which he used from Ariosto to show the degradation of the Red Cross Knight.

Apart from the evidence within the poem and that from the commentary on his major source within the same genre, there is that from the contemporary theory of witchcraft which furnishes an important frame of reference for both Archimago and Duessa. The moral interpretations or allegory found in such episodes is really not much more than a literary extension of the serious writings on the "damned art." As St. Paul emphatically pointed out to the Ephesians, it was not against flesh and blood that the warfaring Christian was pitted, but the machinations of the devil, and one of his major stratagems in the sixteenth century was found in witchcraft.[19] The sin of the Red Cross Knight, then, which has already been described in terms of the sins of the flesh at the natural level must also be considered as a result of the machinations of the devil.

Since the moral responsibility for any act depends on the measure of freedom accorded to the individual will, the gravity

[18] Alcina became a symbol in Du Bellay. See Alexandre Cioranescu, *L'Arioste en France, Des origines à la fin du XVIII siècle* (Paris, 1938), pp. 68-69.

[19] See Reginald Scot, *The Discoverie of Witchcraft*, ed. Summers, p. xxvii; Kittredge, *Witchcraft in Old and New England* (Harvard Univ. Press, 1928), Chaps. II, IV, and XVII; and Robert West, *The Invisible World* (Univ. of Georgia Press, 1939).

of the sin of the Red Cross Knight depends on the extent of
the devil's power to deceive the sons of men through the agency
of witches and magicians. Unfortunately, the answer to this
question is exceptionally complex because it involves both the
devil's power over the physical universe as well as the spiritual
states of those he is subjecting to temptation. Even a brief
examination of the deception of the Red Cross Knight in the
light of contemporary witchcraft, however, adds further historical evidence to the nature of his responsibility.

Although there is no indication in the text that Red Cross
should have suspected Archimago from the outset,[20] his dream
might well have put him on his guard for two reasons: first,
because the devil, finding it difficult to attack the virtuous,
" molests them chiefly in dreams ";[21] and second, because this
dream represented unaccustomed sensual passions for the pure
minded knight and therefore might be of demonic origin.[22]
This was particularly true because witchcraft, however much
its final end might be blasphemy, was rooted in the weakness
of the flesh. In the words of the *Malleus Malificarum*, " All
witchcraft comes from a carnal lust . . ." (p. 47). Traditionally
natural dreams were simply a reminiscence of our daily con-
cerns [23] as represented by Scudamore at the House of Care:

[20] John Deacon and John Walker (*A Dialogicall Discourse of Spirits and Devils*,
London, 1601, p. 234), who cites St. Augustine (*De civit.* lib. 2, cap. 26), clearly
indicate the need for suspicion: " The devil when he entendeth most deeply to
circumuent and deceave the sonnes of Men: then he pretendeth the most *religious*
and holiest shewes of all." Nicolas Remy (*Demonolatry*, trans. Ashwin, ed. Summers, London, 1930, p. 33) notes that the devil frequently deceives us in some form
of righteousness, often assuming the habit of a monk. See Mother Robert Falls,
p. 103, and passim.

[21] [Henricus Institoris]. *Malleus Malificarum*, trans. Summers (London, 1928),
p. 54. This classic work on witchcraft went through six editions between 1576 and
1598 (see pp. xli-xlii) and had an enormous authority in Spenser's lifetime. According to Joost Damhouder, sixteenth century criminologist, it was equal to law:
" Ita recepta est in hac scribendi genere eorum auctoritas ut pro lege apud omnes
habeatur." (Cited Paul Carus, *History of the Devil*, Chicago, 1900, p. 323).
Among other books, Dr. Dee sent a copy to Hopwood, justice of the peace. See
Wallace Notestein, *A History of Witchraft in England from 1558 to 1718* (Washington, 1911), p. 79, n. 14.

[22] See Hunter, " Eve's Demonic Dream," *ELH*, XIII (1946), 260-264. Note,
however, that Professor Hunter misses the full significance of dreams as one of
the devil's few approaches to the virtuous. He does not treat of the special problem of what power the devil may have had over unfallen man or whether the
temptation was the result of a general or special permission of God.

[23] *Ibid.*, p. 260.

"Yet in his soundest sleepe, his dayly feare/ His ydle brains gan busily molest" (IV. v. 43). Unusual dreams, however, were either the result of a distempered state of the body or were of supernatural origin, which, it may be recalled, was the argument between Chauntecleer and Pertelote. Witchcraft, however, could produce this distempered state of the body. The contemporary view of natural dreams is well represented by William Perkins, with a proper Calvinistic touch, who says that they are a means by which a man may recognize his own depravity:

[By dreams] a man may guess at the corruption of his owne heart: and knowe to what sinnes he is most naturally inclined. For looke what men do ordinarily in the day time conceiue and imagine in their corrupt hearts, of the same for the most part, they doe corruptly dreame in the night.[24]

The Red Cross Knight, as we have seen, being pure of heart, starts out of his sleep at the unusual dream (I. i. 49). Since his habitual purity was being so sorely tried by such an unusual dream for him, he might easily have suspected it was of demonic origin.

The knight awakens from his dream only to face the false semblance of Una making advances to him. Neither the treatises on witchcraft nor the text itself are of much help in suggesting how he could have discerned the evil spirit. Such transformations, as in Ariosto, were a commonplace of witchcraft, and they even had a certain national historicity in England through the account of the parentage of King Arthur. According to Geoffrey of Monmouth, Uther Pendragon was transformed by Merlin into the form of Gorlois, husband of the Lady Eigr, and he entered her castle in this enchanted form and slept with her " and that night was conceived Arthyr, son of Ythr." [25] The books on witchcraft are filled with stories of such magic semblances of both the living and the dead, frequently with reference to the key text on the Witch of Endor (I Kings, 28; *AV*, I Sam. 28), and although considerable controversy raged as to whether it was really the body of

---

[24] "A Discourse on the Damned Art of Witchcraft," *Workes* (Cambridge, 1611), III, 624. See also *Batman uppon Bartholome* (London, 1582), fol. 83-84ᵛ for a discussion of dreams.

[25] Ed. Griscom (New York, 1929), pp. 425-427.

Samuel or the devil informing an imitation body, there was general agreement, even among such "scientific" authors as Cotta, that the devil could deceive by assuming whatever shape he pleased.[26] There were some who held that there was always a discernible flaw in the imitation body,[27] but the weight of opinion was against this theory.

In brief, neither the dream nor the appearance of the false Una alone is enough to lead him into sin, and rather than being an innocent victim of such devices, he has considerable ground to suspect witchcraft. The very fact that he tempers his feelings in order to wait "to proue his sence" indicates that as long as he keeps reason in control Archimago cannot bring him into sin. What brings him under the power of Archimago's last trick is his own passions. No man could be tempted by witches beyond his power to resist, with the help of God's grace, of course, because to admit the contrary would be to impugn the freedom of the will. If the knight had been sufficiently strong in faith and immovably chaste in feeling, he would have controlled himself. He falls a victim to witchcraft not because of the inherent power of Archimago to deceive but because of his own weakness. Spenser's final judgment upon him, previously quoted, accuses him of "light misdeeming of her loyaltie."[28]

More light is thrown on the incident by examining contemporary theory about who was subject to such impostures and by what means they were perpetrated. All authorities agreed that the devil's power was dependent on the permissive will of God, and most of them held that this permission was general rather than special,[29] and they solved the problem of evil by the dogma that this power was allowed to him to try the good

[26] Perkins, *Workes*, III, 611-612; Deacon and Walker, p. 121; Nicolas Remy, pp. 33, 43-44, 89-90; Cotta, *The Tryall of Witchcraft* (London, 1616), pp. 32-33.

[27] See West, p. 88. Note, however, that West cites Nicolas Remy, who, in turn, based his work on the testimony of witches on trial, the level of the rationalized folk tradition. As might be expected, this evidence contradicts itself. Compare p. 28 with 43 and 89-90. The other examples which West cites are with one exception the folk story of the cloven hoof found in "The Demon Lover."

[28] Even Professor Whitaker makes an excuse for the Red Cross night's behavior in accepting Duessa, and he cites I. vii. 1 as evidence. It seems to me that the general application of the story to all of us is really a warning on the weakness of our "earthly wit" and not really an excuse for the Red Cross Knight.

[29] West, pp. 95-98.

and punish the wicked.[30] They also agreed that the devil's
power was greatest over the wicked, *especially the lustful*,[31] and
over men of " infirme and weake faith." [32] The exact extent
of his power over the good, which is all important in passing
judgment on the Red Cross Knight, was the subject of some
controversy because it was inextricably bound up with the
principle of the freedom of the will.[33]

Although Calvin denied that the devil had power over those
in grace,[34] most authors took Job and St. Paul as examples of his
attacks on the godly. Perkins, for instance, sufficiently modi-
fied his Calvinism to maintain that, although the best preven-
tive was " to be within the covenant of grace," because such
men are a " thousand fold more free from the power thereof,
then other men " and are " alwais free from the annoyance of
the vilest Witches in the World," still they are subject to witchcraft to a certain extent (*Workes*, III, 696). This was in keeping with the Puritan emphasis on the warfaring Christian. In
the Catholic tradition very little power was allowed the devil
over the virtuous. Discussing certain illusions of the imagination, the *Malleus Malificarum* also says that " all who are de-
luded in this way are in deadly sin," and further: " The devil
can in no way enter the mind or body of any man, nor has the
power to penetrate into the thoughts of anybody, unless such a
person has first become destitute of all holy thoughts, and is
quite bereft and denuded of spiritual contemplation." Those
especially favored by God's grace, especially those *devoted to
chastity*, are free from such machinations of the devil.[35] On
the other hand, in his *Daemonologia* James I warns that " no
man ought to presume so farre as to promise any impunitie to
himself " because even the best, like Job, were tried by the
devil. He mentions, however, the protective value of a strong

[30] Perkins, *Workes*, III, 613; George Gifford, *A Dialogue concerning Witches*
(London, 1603), sig. D[v], cited Notestein, *A History of Witchcraft*, p. 71.

[31] The key text was Tobias 6: 17, and it was not questioned even by those who
denied it a place among canonical books. See West, p. 241, n. 24.

[32] James I, *Works* (London, 1616), pp. 118-119.

[33] For a theological work which carefully distinguishes these points, especially in
relation to the positions of Luther and Calvin, see Francisco Torreblanca, *Daemonologia* (Mainz, 1623), pp. 233-236.

[34] See West, pp. 95 and 241, n. 24.

[35] Pp. 89-94. See also Prierias, *De Strigimagarum* (Rome, 1575), p. 191 ff.

faith.[36] Temptations of the devil through witchcraft, then, are among the ways in which the virtuous are subjected to trial, but those who are strong in faith and devoted to chastity are doubly protected against such temptations.

An examination of the means by which the devil could attack man explains at the natural level why he had so little power over the virtuous. Both as a superior intelligence and as an experienced observer (with six thousand years of research to his credit), the devil had a great knowledge of natural phenomena and considerable power over the physical universe.[37] He could change the balance of the humours in the body and use other physiological means to tempt a man to sin. He could bring back images from the memory and present them to the intellect in such a way that they would appear as present images of the external phenomena received through the senses. He could stir up the organs of the concupiscible and irascible faculties, but he could not touch the will.[38] By such manipulation of the physical constitution of a man's body, the devil was able to increase the temptations where his victim was weakest and generally take advantage of his constitution. The less control the reason had over the lower faculties, the greater the power of the devil over the man. Even at the natural level, then, the devil had little power over the virtuous because in them the reason had the lower faculties well under its control.[39]

From the basic dogma behind witchcraft, that the devil was permitted this power by God in order to try the good and to punish the wicked, we must conclude that the Red Cross Knight is essentially on trial, and furthermore that the power of Archimago and Duessa to deceive him is not great, espe-

---

[36] *Works*, p. 119. See also Prierias, op. cit., p. 189 ff. It was traditional to except magistrates whose duty it was to punish witches. I am omitting such exceptions when they do not bear on the immediate problem of Red Cross. In listing various remedies against witchcraft, Remy (*Demonolatry*, p. 132), exhorts us to use " The shield of solid faith, the sword of the spirit, the helmet of salvation." He also suggests (p. 104) that no man is so good that he may not sometimes slip and become vulnerable. He based this theory on the testimony of a witch who held that if you said your prayers every morning and always washed your hands before going out, you would be free from the molestation of witches!

[37] Perkins, *Works*, III, 610.

[38] See Hunter, *ELH*, XIII (1946): 261-264; West, p. 29; and to both of these may be added the succinct account in Francisco Torreblanca, *Daemonologia* (Mainz, 1623), pp. 233-236.

[39] See *Malleus Malificarum*, p. 54.

cially if he remains chaste in feeling and strong in faith. Spenser first presents him to us as a virtuous, chaste young knight, protected by the armor of a Christian man and in the company of Truth, but at the hour of his trial he fails because he is not sufficiently strong in faith nor confirmed in chastity. At the allegorical level he doubts Truth, and at the literal level he burns in wrath and a sensual jealousy that make him an easy prey to the next temptation of the flesh. In spite of dreams, false apparitions, what appeared the valid testimony of the senses, and the later appeal of what seemed a lady in distress, if the Red Cross Knight had kept passion under the rule of reason, he would not have been started on his way to ruin by the witchcraft of Archimago and Duessa. Rather than furnishing him with excuses, the contemporary theory of witchcraft only supplies further evidence to convict him of moral weakness.

From this evidence it appears that the moral lesson which the deception of the Red Cross Knight by Archimago and Duessa was supposed to teach is thoroughly integrated with both plot and character. The capture of the Red Cross Knight by the charms of Duessa and the force of Orgoglio is the logical outcome of his giving way to passion in the hermitage. Not only does Spenser appear as a more careful artist than might be concluded from Mrs. Bennet's emphasis on the evolutionary aspects of the *Faerie Queene*, but the Red Cross Knight himself emerges less as a wooden allegorical figure and more as a creature of flesh and blood. The integration of the narrative structure with the vigorous moral lesson illustrates further Spenser's mastery of his materials.

The Catholic University of America

VIII

SPENSER AND THE COUNTESS OF LEICESTER

By Charles E. Mounts

The more thoughtfully one reviews the protracted negotiations for marrying Queen Elizabeth to the Duke of Alençon, observing all the while the consistently vigorous and determined opposition offered to this marriage, both in Council and out, by the Earl of Leicester, the more dissatisfied does one become with one of the long accepted theories of Spenserian scholarship.[1] I refer to the celebrated interpretation of *Virgils Gnat* to the effect that sometime later than October, 1579 (when the poet was still considering dedicating *The Shepheardes Calender* to Leicester), Spenser, by means of some version of *Mother Hubberds Tale* that we do not now possess, undertook to " warn " Leicester of the danger presented to his own hopes by the French marriage project and was rewarded for his embarrassing zealousness by the loss of expected patronage and by virtual banishment to Ireland. Not only do we not now believe, as Professor Greenlaw did, that *Mother Hubberds Tale* was " called in " at any date prior to the publication of the *Complaints* volume in 1591, but even the assumption that Spenser could have been so curiously naïve in the declining months of 1579 as to think that his patron needed any such warning seems amply belied by the circumstances. The marriage project had been revived in the summer of 1578, Simier had come to England as a special ambassador in January, 1579, and at the end of June, 1579, Leicester had striven vainly to

---

[1] Symptomatic of a comparatively recent shift in opinion is Leicester Bradner, *Spenser and the Faerie Queene* (Chicago, 1948), pp. 26-27. For earlier expressions of dissatisfaction with the Greenlaw theory, see Harold Stein, *Studies in Spenser's Complaints* (New York, 1934) and Robert Brice Harris, " The Ape in *Mother Hubberds Tale*," *Huntington Library Quarterly*, IV (1940), 191-203. As recently as 1945, however, Spenser's best biographer could still view the theory with respect (Judson, *The Life of Edmund Spenser*, pp. 70-71). The object of the present paper is to discredit it still further and to suggest a substitute solution for some of the problems it seemed to solve.

keep the Queen from signing Alençon's passports. Curiously
enough the very day, October 5, when Spenser dated from
Leicester House the first part of his letter to Harvey, was one
of the days (October 2-8) on which there was constant debate
in the Privy Council over the French marriage.[2] It was at this
critical juncture, if we are to believe Professor Neale, that
Simier launched his most devastating weapon against Leicester— the private revelation to Queen Elizabeth that the man
she had loved and had almost married had long been married
secretly to her own second cousin, Lettice Knollys, widow of
the first Earl of Essex and henceforth to be acknowledged
openly as the Countess of Leicester.[3] Scholarly opinion differs
as to the date of Simier's startling disclosure; it very probably
was made at the beginning of July,[4] but whatever the date,
Spenser can scarcely have felt at any time after July, 1579,
that his patron needed to be prodded into opposing the French
marriage. To the contrary, it must have been apparent to
everyone that Leicester had been doing so all along.

Consequently, though it still seems likely that Spenser's
first draft of *Mother Hubberds Tale* had at least part of its
inspiration in the English opposition to the French marriage
and though the publication of such a poem by Leicester's own
protégé at a time of the Earl's disgrace with the Queen might
have been signally disadvantageous both to the patron and to
the poet, it is obvious that the entire story has not been told.
Professor Greenlaw stated the situation reasonably well when
he observed that " in October, Spenser was at Leicester House,
intimate with the powerful group of men about the great earl,
confident of preferment; by the following April, he has turned
once more to literature. In August he was in Ireland, the dream
over."[5] Like Professor Greenlaw I propose now to offer an
explanation of these circumstances, basing my observations not
upon an unpreserved version of a poem we have no proof that
Leicester ever saw but upon a published poem that it is hardly
conceivable that he did not see—*The Shepheardes Calender*
itself.

[2] *Cal. Salisbury MSS.*, II, 268.

[3] J. E. Neale, *Queen Elizabeth* (New York, 1934), p. 242.

[4] M. W. Wallace, *The Life of Sir Philip Sidney* (Cambridge, 1915), p. 212.

[5] Edwin Greenlaw, "Spenser and the Earl of Leicester," *PMLA*, XXV (1910),
538.

We may be reasonably confident that there was no falling
out between Spenser and his patron until some months after
the *Calender* had appeared in print, certainly not until after
the composition of Spenser's last extant letter to Harvey in
April, 1580, at which time Spenser still was enjoying cordial
relations with Leicester. He writes with reference to his patron:
" His honour never better." Yet that there was indeed some
kind of falling out and that the cause of the trouble was something exceedingly personal are both facts plainly to be inferred
from Spenser's dedication of *Virgils Gnat*:

> Wrong'd, yet not daring to express my paine,
> To you (great Lord) the causer of my care,
> In clowdie teares my case I thus complaine
> Vnto your selfe, that onely priuie are:

Furthermore, it is a matter concerning which the poet is so
painfully embarrassed that he dreads lest it become known:

> But if that any Oedipus unware
> Shall chaunce, through power of some diuining spright,
> To reade the secrete of this riddle rare,
> And knowe the purporte of my euill plight,
> Let him rest pleased with his owne insight,
> Ne further seeke to glose vpon the text:
> For griefe enough it is to grieued wight
> To feele his fault, and not be further vext.[6]

So laden with emotional intensity are these lines that I confess
a certain trepidation, even after these hundreds of years, lest
by trying to play the Oedipus to this riddle, I may still vex
the spirit of my best loved poet. At least there is distinguished
precedent for the attempt, but where Professor Greenlaw
sought the answer in a matter of public policy such as the
French marriage, I shall advance the conjecture that Spenser's
real offense, whether inadvertent or intentional, was a good
deal more personal than that. And at any time in the years
1579 and 1580 there could have been no point on which the
inmost feelings of Robert Dudley were more vulnerable than
his relations, past and present, with his new wife, the former
Lettice Knollys.

---

[6] *The Minor Poems*, II, 83. All quotations from Spenser are from the Johns
Hopkins Variorum edition.

Gossip had linked the names of Leicester and of Elizabeth's fair second cousin as long before as 1565, when she was only twenty-five and the wife of the man who was soon to become the first Earl of Essex. During her husband's absence as Lord Deputy of Ireland between 1573 and 1575 she did not accompany him; to the contrary, she seems to have been present at the festivities at Kenilworth in 1575 and to have entertained the Queen's entourage at Chartley soon thereafter. By the end of 1575, when her husband returned from Ireland, London gossip was already accusing her of having had two children by Leicester.[7] Very possibly the charge was absurd, but Leicester gave further cause for talk when he showed himself anxious in March, 1576, for Essex's return to Ireland. Then at Dublin in September Essex was seized with violent dysentery, suffered heroically for days, and died on September 22, after especially commending his eldest son to the Queen's favor. With such a background the charge of poisoning was inevitable, and though a careful post mortem examinatioin revealed no incriminating evidence whatsoever, it did not help much that the inquest was conducted by Sir Henry Sidney, the brother-in-law of Leicester.

Guilty or not guilty of adultery and murder, however we may judge them, Leicester and Lettice could now indulge their mutual inclination legitimately, though none the less covertly. Professor Wallace quotes a letter presumed to be from Sir Philip Sidney to Leicester on December 16, 1577, in which Sidney wishes to be remembered to his " Lady and aunt," [8] which is all the more interesting when we remember that Lettice was the mother of Penelope Devereux, generally conceded to be the heroine of Sidney's *Astrophel and Stella*. Though later research has thrown doubt on Wallace's assumption that this letter was addressed to Leicester at all, the story of the speedy secret marriage at Kenilworth between the so recently widowed Countess of Essex and Sidney's " singular good lord and uncle " seems virtually undoubted.[9] Apparently, nevertheless, the bride's relatives were not satisfied with whatever cere-

---

[7] Neale, *Queen Elizabeth*, p. 242.

[8] *Life of Sidney*, p. 197. Wallace cites *Harleian MS.* 6992, No. 42.

[9] See Feuillerat, *The Complete Works of Sir Philip Sidney* (Cambridge, 1923), III, 396.

mony had already hallowed the union, and so at Wanstead on
September 21, 1578, took place a second ceremony—like the
first to be kept as long as possible from the knowledge of
the Queen. As we have already seen, that secret was kept
at least until July, 1579—possibly even until October—but
the endeavor to keep it must have filled both the Earl and
his Countess with a greater sensitiveness to gossip than was
usually their wont. And after the blow fell, and the extent of
the Queen's displeasure toward Leicester and hatred toward
" that she-wolf," [10] his wife, had been painfully realized, it
would have been too much to expect that either of these
impetuous, self-willed aristocrats would have brooked for an
instant the sort of sneering personal allusion from a dependent
which one or the other, or both, may have seen—or merely
fancied that he saw—in the March eclogue of *The Shepheardes
Calender*.

What, may we ask, would either the Earl or the Countess of
Leicester have made of such lines as these?

> Tho shall we sporten in delight,
> And learne with Lettice to wexe light,
>   That scornefully lookes askaunce
>
>   (19-21)

Would they have been any more pleased by " Willyes Embleme? "

> To be wise and eke to loue,
> Is graunted scarce to God aboue.

Or by " Thomalins Embleme? "

> Of Hony and of Gaule in loue there is store:
> The Honye is much, but the Gaule is more.

Nor would E. K.'s gloss of *Lettice* as " the name of some country lasse " have been well received by an aristocratic lady at
the time residing in the country because she dared not show
her face at court.[11] As for the gloss of *askaunce* as " askewe or

[10] Milton Waldman, *Elizabeth and Leicester* (Cambridge, Mass., 1945), p. 159.
[11] The fact that, in later years at least, the given name *Lettice* was reasonably
common in England renders all the more unlikely the possibility that Spenser
employed the name intentionally in disparagement of the Countess of Leicester.
On the other hand, I have not been able to discover any earlier use of *Lettice* as a
pastoral name. Michael Drayton's use of it in the ninth eclogue of his *Pastorals*

asquint," the Countess would scarcely have been amused; she
was notoriously a woman of exceeding, if somewhat haughty,
beauty, as her portrait well proves. In fact, it looks a good
deal as though " E. K." were merely up to his usual tricks of
throwing dust in the eyes of the reader. Here then would seem
to be a professional hazard to be faced by the writer of allegorical verses about his contemporaries. If Algrind meant Bishop
Grindal and Syrinx obviously must be Anne Boleyn, who might
this Lettice be? Could it possibly be that she was that notori-
ous beauty who had been carrying on so scandalously with the
Earl of Leicester? And what would the Earl say if he only
knew?

Here, then, in a nutshell is enough dynamite to blow the
poet out of Leicester's favor and into Ireland. It would not be
necessary for him to be proved guilty of deliberately so trifling
with the Countess's name and reputation. Had the March
eclogue been devised in these very terms out of the sheerest
inadvertency,—supposing, for example, that Spenser did not
even know what the great lady's given name was—he could
still scarcely expect to come off scotfree after so egregious a
blunder. Gone were grace and favor, gone in the twinkling of
an eye, and no apology that he could ever make would abolish
the suspicion that the allusion was intentional Indeed, is it
not unlikely that the great lord would even condescend so far
as to put into express terms the reason for the sudden fury
that sent a poet packing? In fact, may not a considerable time
have elapsed before Spenser knew for a certainty just what
had brought down disfavor upon him? If such actually was
the occasion for Leicester's wrath, no wonder Spenser later
expressed himself but sourly in the dedication to *Virgils Gnat.*

Right here I should like to inveigh against a tendency on
the part of even such sound Spenserian scholars as Professor
Judson and Professor Jenkins to explain away the significance
of Spenser's going to Ireland, finding in it no loss of favor at
all, but merely a sort of promotion, a welcome opportunity
to improve his fortunes. To accept this too rosy-colored view
is to discredit Spenser's own most explicit testimony in *Colin
Clout,* lines 180-183:

(1619) presumably derives from Spenser but conveys none of Spenser's moral
opprobrium. See Oxford ed. (1932), II, 566.

Ne gan to cast great lyking to my lore,
And great dislyking to my lucklesse lot:
That banisht had my selfe, like wight forlore,
Into that waste, where I was quite forgot.

These lines commemorative of Ralegh's befriending of Spenser in 1589 are usually considered sincere; yet they are in complete accord with Professor Greenlaw's interpretation of *Virgils Gnat* as a lament and expostulation over the poet's luckless banishment.[12]

Some other arguments have never been sufficiently urged in this connection. The whole tenor of the October eclogue, so recently published, indicates that Spenser was ambitious to succeed, not as some kind of military secretary or colonial planter, but as a poet. As contrasted with London and the Court, what promise did the Savage Island hold out to him in that respect? True it is that he had been a virtual nobody at Leicester House, but with the increasing popularity of his *Calender* (there were two quarto reprintings before he even came back from Ireland with his *Faerie Queene*), did he have nothing but continued nonentity to look forward to—especially if he stayed on the good side of so powerful a patron as Leicester? Finally, have we not entirely overlooked the natural inclinations and preferences of Spenser's young wife? What did removing to Ireland mean to Machabyas Spenser? Granted that her poet-husband needed more income to support a wife as well as himself, can either of the newly married pair, native Londoners as they apparently were, have looked even with equanimity upon such an unexpected development in their lives?

At any rate, we can hardly quarrel with Professor Greenlaw's inference that *Virgils Gnat* was intended in some way to furnish an analogy for the situation existing between Spenser and his former patron. " It will be remembered that the gnat (Spenser) does the shepherd (Leicester) a service by warning

---

[12] Spenser's word *banisht* is probably a poetical exaggeration, anyhow. But what if Spenser, losing out rather violently with Leicester, was rescued, as some already suspect, by the Sidneys (cf. Judson, *Life of Spenser*, p. 71, where the opinion is given that not Leicester but Sir Henry Sidney got Spenser his post with Lord Grey), and sent to a turbulent land where he had not even the slightest desire to go?

him of the snake," says Professor Greenlaw,[13] but I should like
to suggest that the snake may stand, not for the French marriage, but for Leicester's amorous dalliance with the Countess
of Essex. After all, there can be no doubt as to what Spenser
means by " to wexe light "; Red Cross is persuaded by Archimago to think evil of Una and is " Much grieu'd to thinke that
gentle Dame so light." [14] And if the Lettice of the March
eclogue " scornefully lookes askaunce," so does Malecasta, who

> seemed a woman of great bountihed
> And of rare beautye, sauing that askaunce
> Her wanton eyes, ill signes of womanhed,
> Did roll too lightly, and too often glaunce,
> Without regard of grace or comely amenaunce.[15]

Whatever estimate Spenser may have formed of the new
Countess of Leicester by the time he published the *Calender*
in 1579, his complete omission of all mention of her in *The
Ruines of Time*, written in 1590, cannot be without significance.
There Ambrose Dudley, the " good Lord Warwick," who had
died the year before, is warmly praised " That whilste he liued,
was of none enuyde, / And dead is now, as liuing, counted
deare," [16] and his widow Anne Russell receives an entire stanza
of eloquent tribute as a " faire flower of chastitie." The contrast of this pair with Robert Dudley and his wife is startling;
Spenser, only two years after Leicester's death, finds " no man
left to mone / His dolefull fate that late him loued deare " [17]
and is moved to melancholy reflections on the " trustlesse state

---

[13] "Spenser and the Earl of Leicester," *PMLA*, XXV (1910), 538.

[14] *F. Q.*, I, i, 55, 2.

[15] *F. Q.*, III, i, 41, 6-9. It is instructive, at this point, to compare Spenser's
description of Malecasta with the portrait of the Countess reproduced in Waldman's *Elizabeth and Leicester* opposite p. 132. Conjectures are not facts, but any
reasonable conjecture carries with it a train of warrantable speculations. Granted
that in the March eclogue any reference to the Countess is probably unintentional,
need this be the case with a description that did not see print until 1590, especially if Spenser in the meantime had become grievously enlightened as to how the
lewdness of a great lady had infected his own fortunes? Even without any sup-
porting conjecture at all, the similarity between Malecasta's nature and the
scandalous reputation of the Countess is sufficient to make one speculate as to the
possible prototype for Spenser's allegorization of Unchastity. In all contemporary
court society Spenser could have found no better model.

[16] *Ruines of. Time*, 241-2 (*Minor Poems*, II, 43).

[17] *Ibid.*, 192-3.

of miserable men " who vainly think themselves happy " When painted faces with smooth flattering / Doo fawne on you, and your wide praises sing." [18] Beyond all question, Lettice, Countess of Essex, had had one of the most brightly painted of those faces, and where is she? Spenser does not say. Yet it is easy to see why he wasted no melodious stanzas on the virtues of Leicester's widow. The Earl had died on September 4, 1588, and before even a year was up, Lettice, at the age of forty-nine had married Sir Christopher Blount, a twenty-four-year-old boon companion of her own wild son.

The obvious dependence of the March eclogue upon its Alexandrian source undoubtedly justifies the assumption that it carries much less weight of contemporary allusion than do most of the other eclogues in the *Calender*. Yet its very Alexandrianism, as Professor Jones noted, should group it with *Virgils Gnat*, the piece in which Spenser is thought to have lamented the evil plight which befell him because he tried to warn his patron of impending danger.

Unfortunately there seems no certain way of knowing how long Spenser worked upon his eclogues or in what order they were composed. Considering how much young Spenser in 1579 seems to have stood in awe of the great Earl—not quite daring, for example, to dedicate the *Calender* to him—and considering, too, how little he had to gain by deliberately making himself offensive, how much he had to lose, it must seem incredible to everyone that he would have made disparaging references to the lady he knew was his patron's lawfully wedded wife, no matter what he personally thought of her character. Indeed, the very Alexandrianism of the March eclogue suggests the probability that it was composed at Cambridge in his college days, before the idea of the *Calender* as a whole had even occurred to Spenser.[19] Regardless of how, in a frantic attempt to placate the wrath of his patron, Spenser may have rationalized his blunder later on, I am completely skeptical that Spenser ever intended this poem at all seriously as a warning. Though I have no doubt that he privately reprobated the great Earl's reputed dalliance with the Countess of Essex as both morally

---

[18] *Ibid.*, 200-201.
[19] Such, indeed, is Professor Botting's conclusion, *Research Studies of the State College of Washington*, V, 43-61, summarized in *Minor Poems*, I, 614.

culpable and politically dangerous, the March eclogue itself is completely lacking in the requisite moral earnestness. But let us suppose that some months or even years went by after its composition and Spenser suddenly found himself in need of a poem to round out his projected *Calender*. How easy it would be to turn this bit of Cambridge Alexandrianism to the purpose. How characteristic, too, of all Spenser's oft-observed economy in such matters. Knowing, as we also do, how often Spenser was later guilty of carelessness in re-editing materials composed at previous times we may seriously doubt that he ever once gave thought to the gibe about Lettice. Even assuming, as indeed we must, that Spenser must unavoidably have acquired by 1579 some knowledge of the scandalous reputation of the Countess, might he not have remained completely oblivious of the potential dangerousness that lurked in his little poem? Even if he had stopped to realize that the Earl's new wife was named Lettice, and that the name *Lettice* occurred in his poem, might he not have rested secure in the belief that E. K.'s commentary would forestall any untoward interpretation?

There is, of course, an alternative possibility—and it must be faced up to as a possibility no matter how incongruous it may be to the usual conception of a poet long believed to be sage as well as serious—that Spenser actually had become sufficiently emboldened by his convictions to make deliberate allusion to the Countess in his March eclogue and to venture hinting, under cover of frivolity, that the Earl's amorous entanglement was liable to cost him the favor of the Queen. The only evidence that gives color to such a possibility is Spenser's indisputable attempt to square himself with his former patron by the peculiar " argument by analogy " afforded by *Virgils Gnat*. This, however, I prefer to view as a specious rationalization after the fact, and it is possibly significant that, so far as we know, the story accomplished exactly nothing in appeasing the wrath of the Earl. In fact we do not know that Spenser ever even risked sending it to him.

At any rate, in one alternative version or the other, and I have endeavored to make my own preference sufficiently clear, we have here a fairly plausible reconstruction of Spenser's predicament in the summer of 1580, *if the conjecture be true that*

*by the March eclogue he gave grievous personal offense to the
Earl and the Countess of Leicester.* Partial confirmation of the
theory lies in the fact that at the time of publishing the
Calender Spenser was apprehensive that it might provoke
attack on the part of persons envious of his achievement and
consequent expected favor. How else can we account for the
tenor of the lines dedicatory to Sidney?

> And if that Enuie barke at thee,
> As sure it will, for succoure flee
> Vnder the shadow of his wing.[20]

Let us suppose merely that some envious dependent told
Leicester that his wife's name appeared in the March eclogue.
Such a malicious action would have been quite enough to
cost Spenser the patronage of the Earl. Such a possibility not
only supplies a much less tenuous explanation of the sonnet
prefacing *Virgils Gnat*, but compels a new interpretation of the
mystifying personal reference to the Blatant Beast with which
Spenser years later was to end Book Six of *The Faerie Queene*:

> Ne may this homely verse, of many meanest,
> Hope to escape his venemous despite,
> More then my former writs, all were they cleanest
> From blamefull blot, and free from all that wite,
> With which some wicked tongues did it backbite,
> And bring into a mighty Peres displeasure,
> That neuer so deserued to endite.   (VI. xii, 41-7)

To assume, as many have, that the mighty peer referred to in
these lines is Burghley is to accuse Spenser of cravenly back-
tracking from a personal antagonism, probably originating as
early as 1579 in the political opposition of Spenser's patron to
Burghley, intensified later by the poet's trouble over his pension, and consistently declared throughout his poetry. That
he would use the concluding stanza of the 1596 *Faerie Queene*
to beat so ignominious a retreat from all that he had ever
written concerning the Lord Treasurer seems sadly out of character. This is undoubtedly why Professor Heffner felt compelled to say that this stanza is not a recantation, but we are
under no compulsion to agree with Professor Heffner that it is a
further defiance.[21]   A simpler interpretation is that Spenser is

[20] *Minor Poems*, I, 5. See also Footnote 12 above.
[21] *F. Q.* (Variorum ed.), VI, 272.

neither recanting nor defying; he is merely stating a forlorn hope that these latest of his published verses will not get him into trouble as some of his first ones did, when " wicked tongues " brought him quite undeservedly into " a mighty Peres displeasure." This statement of bitter reminiscence needs only to be put beside the sonnet dedicatory to *Virgils Gnat* for us to realize that the mighty peer alluded to was probably not Burghley at all, but Leicester.

Finally, if even for a short while following the publication of the *Calender*, the Dudley, the Sidney, and the Devereux families had any private grounds for suspecting that the March eclogue contained opprobrious references to the Countess of Leicester, mother of Penelope Devereux, might we not ourselves suspect that here lies at least part of the explanation for Sidney's long-remarked faint praise of a work so expressly dedicated to him?

University of Florida

IX

THE PICTORIAL ELEMENT IN SPENSER'S POETRY

By Rudolf Gottfried

" After reading a canto of Spenser two or three days ago to an old lady, between seventy and eighty years of age," Alexander Pope remarked on one occasion, " she said that I had been showing her a gallery of pictures."[1] Old ladies have a way of starting things; and Pope's ripe listener might well be flattered if she were to learn how many critics of a later time have made the same curious estimate of Spenser's art and how often in the last two hundred years her gallery of pictures has been catalogued.

Her point of view was never expressed with more convincing or elaborate self-assurance than by Taine, who wrote in 1856:

This fount of living and changing forms is inexhaustible in Spenser; he is always imaging; it is his specialty. He has but to close his eyes, and apparitions arise; they abound in him, crowd, overflow; in vain he pours them forth; they continually float up, more copious and more dense. . . . Is it possible to refuse credence to a man who paints things for us with such accurate details and in such lively colours? . . . Spenser's characteristic is the vastness and overflow of his picturesque invention. Like Rubens, whatever he creates is beyond the region of all traditions, but complete in all parts, and expresses distinct ideas. As with Rubens, his allegory swells its proportions beyond all rule, and withdraws fancy from all law, except in so far as it is necessary to harmonise forms and colours. . . . Do we find here nothing but fairy land? Yes; here are finished pictures true and complete, composed with a painter's feeling, with choice of tints and outlines; our eyes are delighted by them. This reclining Acrasia has the pose of a goddess, or of one of Titian's courtesans. An Italian artist might copy these gardens, these flowing waters, these sculptured leaves, those wreaths of creeping ivy thick with glossy leaves and fleecy flowers.[2]

But English writers had long anticipated Taine in empha-

[1] Joseph Spence, *Anecdotes . . . from the Conversation of Mr. Pope* (London, 1820), p. 296.
[2] *A History of English Literature*, trans. H. Van Laun (Philadelphia, n. d.), 1. 293, 304, 314, 319.

sizing Spenser's pictorial qualities. A century earlier Joseph Warton compared the author of *The Faerie Queene* with Rubens;[3] and this parallel became almost a maxim with the Romantic critics. Thomas Campbell called Spenser the " Rubens of English poetry ";[4] and Hazlitt developed this idea with his peculiar zest for painting: " In reading these descriptions, one can hardly avoid being reminded of Rubens' allegorical pictures; but the account of Satyrane taming the lion's whelps . . . has even more of the high picturesque character. Nobody but Rubens could have painted the fancy of Spenser."[5] Rubens alone, however, could not long appease an appetite for the picturesque; and Leigh Hunt chucked the whole Louvre into the Spenserian hopper: " I think that if he had not been a great poet, he would have been a great painter; and in that case there is ground for believing that England would have possessed, and in the person of one man, her Claude, her Annibal Caracci, her Correggio, her Titian, her Rembrandt, perhaps even her Raphael. . . . [Spenser's pictures] give the Poet's Poet a claim to a new title,—that of Poet of the Painters "; and Hunt proceeded to hang a gallery of descriptive passages from *The Faerie Queene*, enthusiastically labeling them with the names of Raphael, Correggio, Michelangelo, Giulio Romano, Titian, Guido Reni, Salvator Rosa, Rembrandt, Poussin, Claude Lorraine, and Albano.[6]

After 1856, when Taine had published his oracular endorsement of this conception, it became a fixed point in studies of Spenser's poetry; critics, even good ones, could only repeat it or, at best, refine upon it. Lowell, for example, qualifies a general resemblance of *The Faerie Queene* to Guido Reni by finding " a Teniers-like realism " in one portion of the work, compares a passage in *Muiopotmos* to a painting by Veronese, and spins a web of simile around the poet: " He makes one think always of Venice; for not only in his style Venetian, but as the gallery there [the Accademia] is housed in the shell of an abandoned convent, so his in that of a deserted allegory.

---

[3] Frederic I. Carpenter, *A Reference Guide to Edmund Spenser* (Chicago, 1923), p. 278.

[4] *Ibid.*, p. 256.

[5] *Complete Works*, ed. P. P. Howe (London, 1930). 5. 41-2.

[6] *Imagination and Fancy* (London, 1883), pp. 92-3, 95, 98-116.

And again, as at Venice you swim in a gondola from Gian
Bellini to Titian, and from Titian to Tintoret, so in him, where
other cheer is wanting, the gentle sway of his measure, like the
rhythmical impulse of the oar, floats you lullingly along from
picture to picture." [7] A few years later Aubrey de Vere, in the
taste of his period, again compares Spenser with Guido Reni,
while Edward Dowden decides that the Red Cross Knight
resembles Dürer's engraving of St. George rather than Raphael's
St. Michael.[8] And in 1906 it is not surprising to find Yeats, who
had been educated on late Romantic criticism of this type,
denying that the gardens of *The Faerie Queene* are allegorical
and boldly assuring us that Spenser " seemed always to feel
through the eyes, imagining everything in pictures." [9]

What *is* perhaps surprising is to find that twentieth-century
scholarship, which has frequently plumed itself on having a
new and far more valid comprehension of Spenser's mind and
art, still frequently betrays what is, in effect, the view of Pope's
old lady. " As Dr. Maynadier once pointed out to me," writes
Herbert E. Cory in reference to Red Cross and the dragon,
" the whole setting is quaintly pre-Raphaelite. The hills seem
low and close together and made of pasteboard. Or perhaps
one thinks of Dürer "; and he later tells us, " Some of the large
and impetuously drawn figures of Book Two . . . are limned
with something of the heavy strength which we see in that dead
giant Christ whom Rubens has portrayed in the ' Descent from
the Cross ' in Antwerp." [10] Jefferson B. Fletcher, while depre-
cating the comparison of Spenser to the more atmospheric
painters, bequeaths us a collection of his own choice:

[Trompart's vision of Belphoebe] is a perspective analogous to that
of the Chinese—and Pre-Raphaelite—painter who veins in a leaf
yards distant from the spectator. . . . Spenser's love of crude colors
combined with his sensitiveness to " tactile values " . . . associates
him with the earlier Florentine painters. His maiden queen of the
" April " eclogue of *The Shepheardes Calender* suggests Botticelli's
Primavera as closely as the stanzas of Poliziano which are supposed
to be based on it. To visualize Belphoebe . . . we should look at

---

[7] *Literary Essays* (Cambridge, Mass., n. d.), 4. 309-10, 326-7.
[8] Edmund Spenser, *Complete Works*, ed. A. B. Grosart (London, 1882-1884),
1. 289-90, 330.
[9] Edmund Spenser, *Poems*, selected by W. B. Yeats (Edinburgh, n. d.), p. xlvi.
[10] *Edmund Spenser* (Berkeley, 1917), pp. 106, 109.

Botticelli's Venus new risen from the sea. . . . I believe we should
at least better realize his visual imagery by studying the pictures
of Botticelli, Dürer, and other primitive colorists, and the line en-
gravings of Mantegna, than by reading into his word-pictures the
studied chiaroscuro and atmospheric spaces of Rubens or Veronese
or Turner.[11]

But W. L. Renwick overrides this distinction, discovering in
Spenser elements which resemble not only early painters like
Carpaccio, Fouquet, Uccello, Botticelli, Lippo Lippi, and Ma-
saccio, but also Michelangelo and the masters of chiaroscuro,
Turner and Rubens and Claude Lorraine.[12] Emile Legouis, on
the other hand, finds parallels among painters of the later
Renaissance alone—Titian, Correggio, Primaticcio—and re-
turns to the characteristically Romantic assumption: "Picture
Spenser as a born painter who never held a brush in his hand.
. . . Had he been born in Italy he might have been another
Titian, a second Veronese. In Flanders, he would have anticipated Rubens or Rembrandt. As it was, Fortune made him a
painter in verse, one of the most wonderful that ever lived." [13]

Those to whose generosity and taste we owe our Spenserian
gallery are numberless, but it will suffice to consider only the
last and most interesting of them. In a book published in 1950,
W. B. C. Watkins approaches the subject by attacking his
predecessors: "The Romantics accepted and enjoyed—even
exploited—the pictorial in Spenser, usually content with pointing out compositions in the style of their favorite painters, an
irresistible and incidental pleasure in reading the *Faerie Queene*.
. . . To say, as Hazlitt and Campbell said, that one painter,
Rubens . . . , can do most justice to Spenser is to generalize a
partial kinship ludicrously." [14] For a moment Watkins seems
to be on the verge of a new insight. But in the upshot he reveals
that his quarrel with the Romantics arises merely from their
failure to collect their ludicrous comparisons with sufficient
catholicity:

[The picture of Gluttony is close] to Rubens on the one hand, and
on the other to the powerful grotesqueries of the School of Hierony-

---

[11] *SP*, 14. 158, 162-3.
[12] *Edmund Spenser: An Essay on Renaissance Poetry* (London, 1925), pp. 121-3.
[13] *Spenser* (London, 1926), pp. 102, 112-3, 96.
[14] *Shakespeare and Spenser* (Princeton, 1950), pp. 229, 232.

mus Bosch. . . . Spenser's description of Mount Acidale in its essentials might be an engraving after Mantegna's " Parnassus ".
. . . [The garland pattern of the dancing maidens in Book Six] is found in Botticelli more often than Mantegna, and the final grouping of figures suggests the Three Graces in " La Primavera ". . . .
Comparison of Spenser's various naked girls with snaky hair like golden wire to Botticelli's Venus rising from the sea has been frequent. Less obvious but equally striking is the similarity to Botticelli's " Sleeping Mars " of Spenser's Verdant in the Bower of Bliss.
. . . For a counterpart in painting to Acrasia we must go to Giorgione and Titian. . . . Spenser instinctively dramatizes. A similar desire for drama among later Italians led to the astonishing technique of Michelangelo and the great baroque painters, the later Titian and Tintoretto, from whom stems El Greco. . . . Pastorella among the Brigands is conceived . . . as a painting, showing even the innovation of the candle, like the studies in artificial light which fascinate El Greco . . . , Rembrandt . . . , the French and Dutch Caravaggians, Chardin . . . , and the moderns.[15]

Watkins, in other words, has obviously enjoyed a better course in the history of art than most of his Romantic predecessors had; but his point of view does not differ in any essential way from theirs. Like them, he assumes that Spenser sees the world with the eye of a pictorial artist; that although he does not use the same medium, his descriptions are similar to paintings in content, organization, and effect; and that therefore we can increase our understanding of his poetry by comparing it to the work of well-known painters.

What, it may then be asked, is the validity of these assumptions? or to limit the question, since the last of them is merely a corollary of the other two: did Spenser actually see with the eye of a painter, and are his descriptions actually similar to paintings?

To begin with, it is a striking phenomenon that in spite of all the rhapsodies on the pictorial nature of Spenser's poetry, no artist has ever made a satisfactory illustration of any of his poems. Blake, to be sure, painted a charming water color called " Characters from Spenser's ' Faery Queene ' "; but it is a composite fantasy, not an illustration of any specific scene, and it is pure Blake in style, suggesting nothing which is typical of

[15] *Ibid.*, pp. 234-9, 241.

Spenser.[16] On the other hand, few readers would regret today that Burne-Jones failed to complete the series of panels he designed on the subject of *The Faerie Queene*; and if one may judge from reproductions, the glories of that poem are hardly reflected in the murals which Lee W. Zeigler did not fail to complete in Baltimore a few years ago.[17] The history of the illustrated editions of Spenser begins with his first book, *The Shepheardes Calender* of 1579; but since then there have been only about twenty such editions, and no lover of the poet would care to see more of the kind which have appeared. The truth is that Spenser's poetry is not easy to illustrate, presumably for reasons inherent in the poetry itself.

To this presumption we may add a second: namely, that Spenser cannot, in his time and country, have known much of what we call the Fine Arts. In 1553 the Italian critic Benedetto Varchi, turning the words *ut pictura poesis* to a use never intended by Horace, had expressed the idea that as painting is a kind of silent poetry, so poetry is a kind of painting in language; [18] and some form of this doctrine, which became popular in the sixteenth century, probably reached Spenser. But if he believed that painting and poetry were related arts, the first half of the equation could have little or no meaning for him. The Elizabethans placed a typically Anglo-Saxon emphasis on portraits, the best of which were then miniatures; [19] and the great influx of foreign paintings of other types did not begin before the seventeenth century. Spenser's world, it is true, contained many objects which displayed both English and Continental craftsmanship at their best; and fruitful study has been made of the relationship his poetry reveals with illustrated emblem books, with Tudor architecture, and with the tapestries that hung in noble houses.[20] But as regards painting, with its mature and studied use of line, of color, of composition, of

---

[16] Darrell Figgis, *The Paintings of William Blake* (London, 1925), plate 100.

[17] Watkins, *op. cit.*, p. 232; *Murals Based upon Edmund Spenser's "Faerie Queene"* (Baltimore, 1945), plates.

[18] Horace, *De Arte Poetica*, line 378; Joel E. Spingarn, *A History of Literary Criticism in the Renaissance* (New York, 1899), p. 42.

[19] Recent enthusiasm over the discovery of some Tudor wall paintings only strengthens this point; see A. L. Rowse, *The England of Elizabeth* (New York, 1951), pp. 9-10.

[20] See Frederick Hard, *SP*, 27. 162-85; *Sewanee Review*, 42. 293-310.

chiaroscuro, Spenser must have been almost completely ignorant. The scant references he makes to artists by name betray little knowledge or understanding: in *The Faerie Queene* (3. Pr. 2. 2-3), for example, he refers to Praxiteles as a painter; and in one of his letters (2 April, 1580, postscript), mentioning a projected volume of his poems, he notes that its illustrations, apparently crude woodcuts like those which had just been published in his *Shepheardes Calender*, were so well-made that Michelangelo could not amend the best of them. Even if he intended this to be a joke, it reveals the narrow limits of his artistic education.

In the third place, the belief that Spenser was the Poet of the Painters is belied by his poetry itself. However strong his interest in physical beauty and physical ugliness, and however vivid his occasional observations of the world around him, it can be demonstrated that his visual imagination was subordinate to other faculties and relatively weak.

As evidence of a certain heedlessness which is characteristic of his descriptions, it will not be pedantic to cite a few details. The first of them, paltry as it may appear in itself, is representative: one of the heroes of *The Faerie Queene* sees in the distance a band of savages preparing to sacrifice a naked girl by the light of their fire; but when he has put them to flight and untied her, the complete darkness prevents him from recognizing her as the sweetheart for whom he has been searching all along (*F. Q.* 6. 8. 48-51). Within the space of three stanzas Spenser forgets the picture with which he began.

Again, after describing Ate as a lady of " faire semblance " and " beautie and good grace," the poet tells us that

> Her face most fowle and filthy was to see,
> With squinted eyes contrarie wayes intended,
> And loathly mouth, vnmeete a mouth to bee.

Four stanzas later, realizing the inconsistency, he explains that she had become " As fresh and fragrant as the floure deluce " in order to abuse good knights; but after three cantos Ate has, without reason or explanation, turned into a hag again (*F. Q.* 4. 1. 17. 6-7, 27. 1-3, 31. 5-9; 4. 4. 9-10). Clearly, Spenser either fails to visualize his character's appearance or does not consider it necessary that his reader should do so.

Or to take a case where his ineptitude may well be deliberate: the butterfly who is the hero of *Muiopotmos* is described as dressed in the shaggy hide of a wild beast which he had slain, a garment which made him look like Hercules wearing his lion skin (*Mui*. 65-72). If the absurdity is suitable to a mock-heroic poem of this kind, it is significant that Spenser subordinates the pictorial element to a literary idea.

But the best-known and one of the most telling of his lapses occurs on the very threshhold of *The Faerie Queene* (1.1.1-6), where he describes a party of three wayfarers: Red Cross spurring forward on his angry steed, Una riding quite slowly on a humble ass, and a dwarf who lags on foot behind them both. This party, as any freshman is able to see, cannot remain a party long; and yet the poet assures us that they are traveling together on one quest. How account for the visual impossibility? The explanation lies in the moral meaning of the figures: Red Cross spurs forward because he represents Religious Zeal, Una rides slowly as becomes the quality of Truth, and the dwarf must lag behind, being the symbol of Prudence. In general, we may say, Spenser subordinates the pictorial element to the moral allegory.

The force of this generalization reappears in the same canto, where we are told of Red Cross in the Cave of Error:

> his glistring armor made
> A litle glooming light, much like a shade.
>
> (*F. Q.* 1.1.14.4-5)

Here the enthusiastic connoisseur, rejoicing in his acquisition, is wont to find a remarkable affinity to Rembrandt; but the figure of his hero shining in the absolute blackness of the Cave has far more of an allegorical than of a pictorial importance for Spenser, who carefully tells us a few lines earlier that "Vertue giues her selfe light, through darkenesse for to wade" (1.1. 12.9).

A preference for imagery involving light or dark or a contrast between the two, it has been frequently observed, appears throughout Spenser's poetry; yet this preference is only an expression of the strong moral bent of his mind, a corollary of the moral light and dark of which he feels our life is made. And a similar relation is evident when we consider his palette. Given his reputation as a word-painter, it is surprising that he should not mention colors more often than he does, while those which he uses most frequently are primary and unsophisticated—gold, red, white, black, green; [21] and the crudity of his choice in many cases reflects an allegorical purport. When, for example, he dresses Faith in white, Hope in blue, and Charity in yellow, he is merely following an emblematic convention (*F. Q.* 1. 10. 13-30); he heeds, not the colors themselves, but the meaning traditionally associated with them.

Spenser's dependence on allegory, we should immediately add, assists as well as limits his descriptive art. If the moral meaning often replaces the purely visual elements, there are also occasions when the intensity of that meaning produces the most vivid pictorial details: I have in mind the terrifying description which precedes the argument between Red Cross and Despair (*F. Q.* 1. 9. 33-6). But even here the success of the picture is obviously due to the ferment of thought and feeling which the idea of suicide arouses in the poet; the very power of the imagery reveals that it is subordinate to a heightened allegory.

Furthermore, allegory cannot provide the constructive element which is lacking in Spenser's visual imagination. His critics have made much of the great processions, or pageants, which appear at various points in *The Faerie Queene*: the perambulation of the Seven Deadly Sins, the masque of Cupid, the marriage of the Thames and Medway, and Mutability's procession of the months and seasons. But if these pageants reflect some pictorial tradition, perhaps derived from the woodcuts or the tapestries which illustrated Petrarch's *Triumphs*, they are also weak in pictorial composition. Each of them consists of a series of separate groups or single figures, and Spenser's eye does not embrace the movement of the whole; he sees them one by one, as if they were passing by outside a narrow door. The deficiency, of course, does not really diminish the poetic value of these passages since they still have an allegorical unity which any right-minded reader can appreciate. Nevertheless, it is a deficiency; and when Spenser attempts, on one occasion, to describe a figure at great length, without the firm support of a continuous moral intention, the result is not satisfactory: he devotes eighty-one lines to the physical charms of Belphoebe, running through them in the following order—her rosy complexion, her bright eyes, her ivory forehead, her sweet voice, her gracious eyelids, her heavenly face, her silken dress, her gilded boots, her stately legs, her sharp spear, her gay bow, her dainty breasts, and her yellow hair (*F. Q. 2. 3. 22-30*). This is merely a catalogue of flattering details; and even Queen Elizabeth, who was supposed to identify Belphoebe with herself, can hardly have regarded it as an impressive portrait.

The pictorial interest, it is thus clear, is actually a minor ingredient of Spenser's art, an adjunct of that intellectual and, in the widest sense, reflective content which lies at the center of his poetry. His pictorial imagery, conspicuous though it may be in such episodes as the Bower of Bliss, is only a kind of commentary on that essential text.

And indeed, if we turn to the sensuous enchantments of his poetry, charms which it would be folly to deny, they will be seen, generally speaking, to consist of something beside pictures, even when it is a question of the so-called pictures themselves. To cite one of those brief descriptions which are as characteristic of *The Faerie Queene* as the longer, set pieces, Spenser writes of Timon's house among the mountains of North Wales:

> His dwelling is low in a valley greene,
> Vnder the foot of *Rauran* mossy hore,
> From whence the riuer *Dee* as siluer cleene
> His tombling billowes rolls with gentle rore. (1.9.4.5-8)

The reader's mind, I think, responds to these lines in a significant way. It visualizes a merely typical landscape, without precise detail or striking form; and yet there is no doubt that the passage also stimulates the imagination. How? Obviously, by its sound and movement. The lines are a triumphant case of verbal melody, whose formal pattern melts into the tumbling river's gentle roar.

The truth is that nine-tenths of Spenser's imagery is addressed to the ear rather than the eye, and therefore the picture galleries which some would-be curators have gathered from his work inevitably misrepresent the character of the whole. To cull descriptive passages out of *The Faerie Queene* is to rob

Spenser of the two elements from which his masterpiece derives its finest appeal: his continuous yet ever-varying music and that sober embodiment of his reflections on our human problems which he called his " continued Allegory." All that such an anthology can give us is a fallacious sense that the pictorial element is an important, if not the most important, aspect of his poetry.

But Spenser himself did not misunderstand the nature of his craft. In one of the conspicuous introductory stanzas of *The Faerie Queene* he alludes to a poet's wit, who

passeth Painter farre
In picturing the parts of beautie daint.   (3. Pr. 2. 6-7)

He can hardly have believed that poetry, which he regarded as the superior art, could or should imitate painting; he would, I feel sure, have deeply resented that misconceived esteem which he enjoys as Poet of the Painters.

Indiana University